DINOSAURS *and* OTHER ANCIENT ANIMALS *of* BIG BEND

꘎꘎꘎

The Corrie Herring Hooks Series

DINOSAURS *and* OTHER ANCIENT ANIMALS *of* BIG BEND

Cindi Sirois Collins & *Asher Elbein*

ILLUSTRATIONS by JULIUS CSOTONYI

UNIVERSITY *of* TEXAS PRESS

Austin

Requests for permission to reproduce material from this work should be sent to:
Permissions
University of Texas Press
P.O. Box 7819
Austin, TX 78713-7819
utpress.utexas.edu/rp-form

∞ The paper used in this book meets the minimum requirements of
ANSI/NISO Z39.48-1992 (R1997) (Permanence of Paper).

Library of Congress Cataloging-in-Publication Data

Names: Collins, Cindi Sirois, author. | Elbein, Asher, author. | Csotonyi, Julius,
    1973– illustrator.
Title: Dinosaurs and ancient animals of Big Bend / Cindi Sirois Collins and Asher
    Elbein ; illustrations by Julius Csotonyi.
Other titles: Corrie Herring Hooks series.
Description: First edition. | Austin : University of Texas Press, 2023. | Series: Corrie
    Herring Hooks series | Includes bibliographical references and index.
Identifiers: LCCN 2022025719
ISBN 978-1-4773-2717-3 (hardcover)
ISBN 978-1-4773-2463-9 (paperback)
ISBN 978-1-4773-2718-0 (pdf)
ISBN 978-1-4773-2719-7 (epub)
Subjects: LCSH: Dinosaurs—Texas—Big Bend Region—Identification. | Fossils—
    Texas—Big Bend Region—History. | Biotic communities—Texas—Big Bend
    Region—History. | LCGFT: Field guides.
Classification: LCC QE861.8.T42 C65 2023 | DDC 560.9764/93—dc23/
    eng20221202
LC record available at https://lccn.loc.gov/2022025719
doi:10.7560/327173

Book design by Endpaper Studio
Typeset in Monotype Bulmer and Brandon Text

I dedicate this book to my loving, supportive, and patient husband, Jack Collins. Through the past four years he watched me drag my laptop and bag o' research everywhere for fear of house fires, etc. Thank you, Jack, you are so loved.
—Cindi

To all those who have walked Big Bend with their eyes on the ground, trying to peer back in time.
—Asher

The full significance of Late Cretaceous faunal differentiation will become clear only after the faunas become known in greater detail.
—Timothy Rowe et al., 1992

Here is our contribution toward that goal.

CONTENTS

INTRODUCTION

THERE'S NO PLACE IN THE UNITED STATES QUITE LIKE BIG Bend National Park. Stretching 801,163 acres across the Chihuahuan Desert, bordered by the muddy sweep of the Rio Grande, the park's boundaries include sweeping hillsides of cactus and volcanic rock, riparian wetlands, and the alpine relict forests of the Chisos Mountains. With 150 miles of trails for day hiking and backpacking trips, it is the largest spread of roadless land in Texas. The dramatic landscapes, wildlife, and specialized vegetation taken together have been called the state's "Gift to the Nation."

The park might also be fairly called the state's Gift to Paleontology. From the mighty walls of Santa Elena Canyon to the desert bluffs of the Aguja Formation and the white banks of the Banta Shut-In, the rocks of the park teem with millions of years' worth of fossils. Many of them have been gathered in the park's Fossil Discovery Exhibit, where visitors can encounter everything from the skulls of dinosaurs to the delicate remnants of ancient plants.

Many of those visitors have questions. Why, they wonder, are there fish fossils in the desert? What sorts of animals were these, with wingspans the size of a small plane, or femurs the size of men? How could one place change so much, even over such a long span of time? And what do all of those tongue-twisting names *mean*?

This book is meant to answer those questions—and many more.

HOW TO USE THIS BOOK

Until now, the fossil history of Big Bend has never been collected in one volume for general readers. This book is designed to fill that gap and to serve as a road map to the fascinating layers of prehistory throughout the park. But even a road map needs a map key.

Chapter 1, "Fossil Hunting in Big Bend," presents a brief account of the history of Big Bend paleontology, fossil displays in the park, and how fossils are created. The second chapter, "The March of Time in Big Bend," tells the story of how the park's landscape took shape over millions of years of draining seas, rising mountains, and erupting volcanoes, like viewing nearly 95 million years of history on fast-forward.

From there, the book slows down to examine each of these vanished ecosystems in turn. Chapters 3, 4, 5, and 6 contain a thought experiment in the form of a time traveler's field notes, or a dispatch of nature writing, by a visitor to each formation in the park as it existed in the Late Cretaceous Period or the Cenozoic Era, up to a mere 100,000 years ago. Drawing from paleontological data and informed speculation, these experiences sample a variety of seasons and track the movement of the seas across the park's formations, to help you imagine yourself in the past.

Within the chapters, the broader families of animals known from each formation are described, introducing important groups in a rough phylogenetic order. Each visit to a formation concludes with a field guide to the notable animal species of that ecosystem. These last sections contain a brief physical description of the animal, a discussion of where the fossils were found and the animal's diet, and details on ecology and natural history in an easy-to-read format. In each species profile, we provide a pronunciation guide: capitalized syllables are emphasized over uncapitalized syllables.

DINOSAURS *and* OTHER ANCIENT ANIMALS *of* BIG BEND

⌐⌐⌐

~~cʊ~ 1 ~~ɔɔ~~

FOSSIL HUNTING
in BIG BEND

FOSSILS ARE THE BODY OR TRACE REMAINS OF PREHISTORIC life, a category that includes everything from the tiniest bit of pollen to the largest dinosaur bones. Any such trace from more than 10,000 years ago counts as a fossil. The name comes from the Latin word *fossilis*, meaning "dug up," which many fossils are. They are found typically in sedimentary-rock layers of clay, silt, sand, mud, or pebbles. These layers—each of which has a specific age—are called "members." A collection of members from the same general geographic area and time period is called a "formation," such as the Aguja Formation, or any of the others discussed in this book.

How does fossilization happen, though? For that, we have to look at taphonomy (from the Greek for "burial law"), the study of all of the processes that occur between a living thing's death and its final preservation in the rock.

CREATING BODY FOSSILS

Usually, when a plant or animal dies, that's the end of it. Most things that die are devoured by other organisms, through either scavenging or decay, and their remnants are eventually recycled back into the ecosystem.

Sometimes, though, the remains of an organism are buried where scavengers and decay-causing organisms can't get at them. If the burial happens early enough, the majority of the remains may be protected. Other times, burial occurs late in the process, leaving only teeth or a few scattered bones. Either way, the remains of the organism are trapped in sediment, which—over millions of years—compacts into rock. The fossil-to-be then usually goes through permineralization, a process in which water full of dissolved minerals saturates the pores and tissues of the remains. The minerals replace the original cells, leaving behind a rocky remnant of the original organic material. After millions of years, these rocky remnants or fossils erode out of a hillside to be discovered and excavated.

The most familiar results of this process are known as body fossils. That's the kind of fossil you're probably thinking about right now: the hard parts of an organism, like teeth, bones, and shells. They are common largely because the hard parts of an organism are the toughest and therefore are more likely to be buried and eventually fossilized. Even then, the creation of a fossil requires a lot of luck. Before the hard parts are buried, storms, floods, or high-energy river currents usually cause skeletons to fall apart (disarticulate) and be transported away from the original place of death. They can be fragmented further into smaller pieces or be physically worn down as they rub against each other or the sediments around them. Many of Big Bend's most spectacular animal remains are body fossils. For example, *Alamosaurus*, one of the last surviving long-necked dinosaurs, is known for large disarticulated parts, such as colossal limbs, massive pelvic bones, and its immensely long neck and tail vertebrae.

The same basic processes that created the body fossils of dinosaurs also created microfossils, which can be seen only with a scanning or transmission electron microscope. Microfossils include the abundant tiny bones of animals as well as plants, bacteria, protists, pollen, spores, and more that existed on land and in water around the world for millions of years. All are smaller than the period at the end of this sentence.

PRESERVING SOFT TISSUES

Body fossils are rare, but fossils that preserve soft tissues—skin, muscle, and connective tissue—are even rarer. Soft tissue is preserved only when an organism is quickly buried and sealed, preventing the growth of bacteria. That tends to happen in places like glacial ice and tar pits, in the oxygen-starved bottoms of lakes or streams, at the sites of volcanic ash-falls, and in water with extremely high or low pH, such as peat bogs and swamps. Under those conditions, when everything happens just right, a soft-tissue fossil can be created.

Sometimes soft tissue is preserved through a process called carbonization. All living things contain carbon, hydrogen, oxygen, and nitrogen. When an organism is buried in the sediment, the hydrogen, oxygen, and nitrogen vaporize or dissolve, leaving only a shiny film of black or brown carbon on the rock's surface. The film, however, can be astonishingly detailed. For instance, the remains of carbonized feathers can contain clues to the original colors of the living animal.

In other cases, researchers are lucky enough to find skin impressions—molds that contain the preserved impressions of an animal's flesh. In dinosaurs, such impressions most famously come from hadrosaurs. One discovered in Big Bend, in the Javelina Formation, was the second occurrence of skin impressions in Texas and a first for the park.

There is another way to make soft-tissue fossils. Sometimes pools of resin—a thick, sticky saplike substance that comes from the bark of conifer trees—will trap insects, seeds, and small vertebrates. When the resin hardens and is buried, it can turn into a beautiful stone called amber. Protected from the passage of time, items preserved in amber look precisely as they did when they were entombed. Although amber has been found in Big Bend, none of it contains any critters—yet.

MAKING AN IMPRESSION

Some fossils are created simply by the everyday actions of animals. Called ichnofossils, or trace fossils, they include footprints, borings, gastroliths, nests, and coprolites. One example is burrows—tunnels made by various sorts of animals—which can be flooded with different sorts of sediments, preserving them. Preserved burrows can give paleontologists evidence of plant and animal materials, water depth, and oxygen content present at the time of the burrow formation. In Big Bend, five different types of marine burrows have been found in the Boquillas Formation and one freshwater burrow has been found in the Aguja Formation.

TELLING TIME

Fossils are also the biological timekeepers of this geological timescale. Segments of Earth's history are represented by index fossils, the appearance and disappearance of which help scientists keep track of the ages of rock layers (known as biostratigraphy). To serve as an index, the type of fossil has to be globally distributed, easy to recognize, and abundant. The best index fossils come from species that evolve quickly and survive for only a short period of time. Some index fossils of Big Bend are ammonites (such as *Allocrioceras hazzardi*) and species of the enormous *Inoceramus* clams.

ARRANGING LIFE

How do scientists know which fossil animals are related to others? That question defines the complex and frustrating field of taxonomy, the science of working out family relationships among animals. You've probably heard the word *species* before, but that's just one part of an entire taxonomic filing system used to work out relationships between animals living and dead.

The bones of this filing system were invented by the Swedish naturalist Carl Linnaeus in 1735. Before Linnaeus, there were no standard and widely accepted systems for arranging or naming animals. Linnaeus used a system of nesting boxes: Kingdom, Phylum, Class, Order, Family, Genus, Species. For example, you, the person reading this book, would be classified as an animal in the Kingdom Animalia, not a plant, fungus, or bacterium. Within the animal kingdom, you are in the Phylum Chordata, since you have a backbone; in the Class Mammalia, since you're a mammal; in the Order Primates, since our family is most closely related to apes and monkeys; in the Family Hominidae, containing humans and our direct and indirect relatives, such as *Australopithecus;* in the Genus *Homo,* meaning the group of human species like Neanderthals and ourselves; and, finally, you belong to the Species *sapiens,* the specific interbreeding population of all modern humans.

Another system—often used somewhat in tandem with Linnean taxonomy—is cladistics, which sorts animals according to the proportion of measurable characteristics that they have in common. A clade is any group of animals that have evolved from a common ancestor. Cladistics also is arranged as a series of nesting brackets, without sticking strictly to the Linnean framework. For example, the group that contains everything more closely related to chimpanzees and humans than to gorillas is a clade.

These are neat systems in theory, and they tend to work acceptably well; but like all human-created systems, they can get messy when put into practice. For example, there isn't a clear, systematic consensus on precisely what counts as a species. What happens when multiple populations look different but occasionally interbreed?

Making classification still messier, tools like genetic analysis, used to study modern species, aren't generally available for fossil remains. Paleontologists instead have to rely on potentially misleading features of anatomy in order to sort animals. Species can be accidentally named twice. Fossils from one species can be misidentified as belonging to another. Experts can argue for years about where a given animal belongs in the tree of life. Taxonomy, therefore, is a best guess about the identity and relationships of living things, constantly evolving as new evidence is found, and a lot of features are still up for debate.

In this book, each notable species we describe will be classified by order and family. If orders or families aren't recognized, for whatever reason, we'll use clades. We'll also talk a little bit about taxonomic wrangling if it sheds light on how people have tried to make sense of fossil remains when they come across them.

TRACING THE HISTORY OF BIG BEND PALEONTOLOGY

When the first native peoples came to Big Bend thousands of years ago, they likely found fossils eroding out of the rock layers. Just what those original wanderers thought of the fossils has not come down to us, but subsequent indigenous peoples who inhabited the region—among them the Mescalero Apache and the Nꭒmꭒnꭒꭒ (Comanche)—were actively interested in the remains they found in other parts of their traditional lands and incorporated discoveries into their traditional knowledge. Unfortunately, none of that knowledge from the Big Bend area was ever formally recorded.

The landscape's wealth of prehistoric material first came to the attention of Western science through Anglo settlers like William H. Emory, a major in the US Army, who, in the aftermath of the bloody Mexican-American War, led the Mexican Boundary Survey of 1848–1853 to map the newly conquered land. His survey was one of the first in the remote region of the Rio Grande; the tallest peak in the park, Emory Peak, was named in his honor.

The first survey of the region's paleontology and geology was carried out by Johan Udden. In 1907 he noted the discoveries of "saurian bones" of hadrosaurs and ceratopsids and a giant alligatoroid that was "new to science." He named the Boquillas Formation and the "sunken block" where the Chisos Mountains are located.

In 1933, in the depths of the Great Depression, the Texas Legislature established Texas Canyons State Park on fifteen sections of land near the canyons of Santa Elena, Boquillas, and Mariscal. Later that year it was renamed Big Bend State Park. In January of 1934, the National Park Service evaluated the site and recommended that it become a national park and that the Civilian Conservation Corps work on the park infrastructure.

A year later, President Franklin D. Roosevelt's New Deal formally created the Works Progress Administration (WPA), an agency designed to put millions of unemployed men to work during the economic catastrophe of the Depression. From 1938 to 1939, a handful of men worked at three fossil quarries in Big Bend, where they were overseen by William S. Strain, then a new professor at the Texas College of Mines and Mineralogy (now UT–El Paso). Dr. Strain had dreams of finding a complete dinosaur to mount in the school's museum. Although the WPA excavation collected 500 bones in almost 3,000 cubic yards (2,294 cubic meters) of rock, Dr. Strain's complete dinosaur skeleton eluded him. Fully intact fossil skeletons were and are the exception in this area, not the rule.

The fossils uncovered at Strain's digs soon attracted America's foremost fossil hunter of the time, Barnum Brown, a man whose flamboyant manner—along with his discovery of *Tyrannosaurus rex* and numerous other species—earned him the nickname Mr. Bones. In the summer of 1940, Dr. Brown, along with his colleague and friend Roland "R.T." Bird, came to the park to prospect for dinosaur remains. They drove over the gullies and bluffs in an old Ford delivery truck, pushing it whenever it broke down, which was often. Dr. Brown had no more luck than Strain when it came to finding complete fossil remains. "If I should find a whole bone," he complained to Bird, "I would not know what to do with it" (Bird, 1985).

Brown's excavations, however, gave the park some of its most famous fossil discoveries. Along with the crushed skull of the ankylosaur *Edmontonia* and the partial skeleton of a horned ceratopsian, Brown and Bird uncovered the immense neck vertebrae of a giant sauropod dinosaur called *Alamosaurus* and the partial jawbones of a huge alligator *Deinosuchus*. It was a remarkably successful expedition for Dr. Brown, and also his last. The outbreak of World War II and his poor health would prevent him from making another field expedition.

In 1944 Congress formally established Big Bend National Park, and Ross A. Maxwell was named its first superintendent in 1945. As a geologist, he felt that he needed to take note of the rocks, formations, and fossils within the park to lay the foundation for the future. In 1969, Maxwell—along with geologists Roy T. Hazzard and John T. Lonsdale, and paleontologist Jack A. Wilson—completed a thorough inventory of the park's geology, which is still being used by today's scientists.

The science of paleontology in Big Bend owes a particular debt to two researchers, John A. "Jack" Wilson (1914–2008) and Wann Langston Jr. (1921–2013). They established academic programs and dynasties that continue to this day.

Dr. Wilson—who eventually served as the president of the Society of Vertebrate Paleontology—joined the University of Texas at Austin in 1946. He dedicated himself to the study of the park's geological formations, with a particular focus on the mammals of the Paleocene, Eocene, and Miocene. In 1949, he was the first to organize UT's fossils in one place, creating the Vertebrate Paleontology Laboratory (VPL); he served as its first director until 1967. By the 1950s, he was leading students on digs in the park, an activity he pursued even after his retirement in 1976. His most noted discovery was the skull of an early primate, *Rooneyia viejaensis*. He is also notable for establishing the park's first permanent in-ground fossil display. (More on that later.)

Dr. Wilson convinced Dr. Langston, also a paleontology professor at the University of Texas, to go to Big Bend to focus his attention on the Cretaceous reptiles. Langston became another important contributor to Big Bend paleontology with his interest in the pterosaurs found in the park. Langston and Wilson found and studied many fossils in their time and together found a more complete *Deinosuchus* skull. Dr. Langston also recovered multiple new *Alamosaurus* remains, including a femur that was as tall as he was and an articulated torso that was, he later crowed, "laid out on its back for all to see" (Lehman and Busbey 2007). He also found the most pterosaur fossils in the park so far. Dr. Langston became the director of the VPL when Dr. Wilson retired in 1969.

Paleontologists taught by those two icons of the field soon set to work excavating the park's fossil riches—from giant animals to miniature ones. In 1971, paleontologist Douglas A. Lawson found a "long, hollow thin-walled bone" that he recognized as coming from the wing of a giant pterosaur (Lawson 1975). His discovery was confirmed by his professor, Dr. Langston. Lawson named the species *Quetzalcoatlus northropi*, and it soon became an icon of Texas prehistory.

Over the course of the 1970s, Judith A. Schiebout, as a graduate student working with Dr. Wilson, introduced screen washing to Big Bend in her search for mammals from the Black Peaks Formation, a period during and after the extinction of the dinosaurs. The technique—which uses mesh screens to sieve out tiny fossils such as mammal teeth and bones—has brought many species of small extinct animals to light, helping to create a more complete picture of vanished ecosystems.

Throughout the last three decades, paleontologists have

uncovered more remains from Big Bend's most iconic species, as well as numerous new animals. Paleontologist Margaret S. Stevens, along with her husband, geologist James B. Stevens, explored and named new outcrops of the Devil's Graveyard and Banta Shut-In Formations. There they discovered new species of extinct mammals and reptiles in and out of the park.

One of Dr. Schiebout's students, Julia T. Sankey, used the screen-washing technique in the Cretaceous sediments of the Aguja Formation, discovering turtle fossils, dinosaur eggshell fragments, and teeth from dinosaurs, including the theropod *Richardoestesia isosceles*. The research team of Thomas M. Lehman (one of Langston's former students) and Steven L. Wick (the park's former paleo technician) has added turtles like *Chupacabrachelys* and *Terlinguachelys* and horned dinosaurs like *Agujaceratops* and *Bravoceratops* to Big Bend's prehistoric fauna.

Dr. Strain's original quarries in 1938–1939 have contributed important new discoveries, such as a large ceratopsian bone bed, and Thomas Lehman also took part in the discovery of *Aquilarhinus palimentus*, a hump-nosed hadrosaur. At the same time, researchers have made increasing use of important small organic fossils called palynofossils (pollen, spores, and marine microfossils) to understand the paleoenvironments of the Big Bend region.

By 2015, fossils from more than 1,200 plant, 450 bird, 56 reptile, and 75 mammal species had been found in the park. The prehistoric wealth of Big Bend shows no sign of running dry, and every field season holds the promise of new discoveries.

DISPLAYING FOSSILS IN BIG BEND

Most people interact with fossils through museum displays, which give us a chance to see accumulated paleontological knowledge in one place. The history of such fossil displays in Big Bend did not have an auspicious beginning. In 1933 the Civilian Conservation Corps built a museum to house the fossils found in what was then Big Bend State Park, but on Christmas Eve 1941, a fire broke out that completely destroyed the building. All of its fossils were lost, including the park's only known mammoth teeth and saber-toothed cat fossils.

While Ross Maxwell, the national park's superintendent, was a geologist who had long been fascinated by the park's paleontological riches, the park spent over a decade without a fossil display. It wasn't until 1957 that Dr. Jack Wilson established the first exhibit of fossil bones. Its use of actual fossils made it the first of its kind in both Texas and the National Park System. Dr. Wilson wanted people to see what the scientists saw when they first discovered a fossil. For 30 years, fossils of *Hyracotherium*, a horse ancestor, and *Coryphodon*, a large hippolike animal that lived during the Eocene, about 55 million years ago (55 mya), were displayed— without glass—for the public. Over the decades, the *Coryphodon* lost a couple of teeth to visitors. In the 1990s, the Fossil Bone Exhibit was moved to accommodate visitors with disabilities. In the intervening years, however, with considerable turnover among the park staff, an important feature of the exhibit was forgotten—that the bones in the exhibit were real fossils, not models. After the park staff tried to remove what they mistakenly believed to be fossil casts, the remains of the extremely fragile fossils were carefully rescued and replaced with replicas.

By the 2000s, the display was showing its age. Park geologist Donald Corrick, in his twenty-plus years at Big Bend, had longed for a more elaborate fossil exhibit that would pay tribute to the park's fossil treasures. Corrick and Steven Wick, the park's paleontological technician at the time, designed a new, more hands-on exhibit that would walk visitors of all ages through the park's vanished ecosystems.

Funded by the Big Bend Conservancy, the National Park Foundation, and a constellation of public and private donors, the Fossil Discovery Exhibit began construction in 2016. The installation covered 3,000 square feet (279 square meters) and opened in January of 2017, featuring skeleton casts, packed fossil display cases, and beautiful murals by paleoartists Julius Csotonyi and Alexandra Lefort. Csotonyi would later go on to provide illustrations for this book.

VISITING THE FOSSIL DISCOVERY EXHIBIT

Start at Panther Junction Park Headquarters on Highway 385 and head north; the exhibit is located on the right side of the road 8 miles (12.8 kilometers) north toward the Persimmon Gap Entrance. The exhibit meets the Universally Accessible standard for wheelchairs and contains large-print pamphlets and touchable displays for those with vision impairment. It can be visited from dawn until dusk any day the park is open.

COLLECTING FOSSILS PRIVATELY IN BIG BEND

It is common to look at interesting fossils and want to own one. Although fossil collecting is legal on private land with the owner's permission, the National Park Service and the United States Bureau of Land Management flatly forbid commercial or private collection of paleontological resources on public lands. That includes places such as federal and state parks, monuments, and US Interstate road cuts.

According to the Paleontological Resources Preservation Act (PRPA) of 2009, a permit is required to legally collect, tamper with, sell, or hold fossils collected on public land; punishment for breaking the law involves hefty fines and potential jail time.

To make this as clear as possible: *Do not attempt to collect fossils in Big Bend National Park as a private citizen if you do not have a permit.*

If you do find a fossil while out hiking in the park, take a picture, or note the location as best you can, and report it to a park official.

∽৩ 2 ৩∽
THE MARCH *of* TIME
in BIG BEND

CONSIDER, FOR A MOMENT, THE PASSAGE OF TIME. A HUMAN life span—if that human is very lucky—is about a hundred years. Two such life spans encompass the history of Texas as a state, and three the time that the United States has existed as an independent country. Ten incredibly long-lived humans, one after another, will witness a thousand years. Imagine the number of human lifetimes contained within a million years.

Then consider that Big Bend has rocks that date back over a hundred million years.

From the time the first fossils in the park were laid down, enough time has passed for a continental sea to become a desert, each successive environment leaving its trace in pages of rock. It is a depth of time that is difficult to grasp—time enough for mountains to rise and oceans to drain, for the landscapes we think of as static to shift and flow like water.

One can compare that time to a history text, wrote geologist Ross Maxwell, the first superintendent of Big Bend National Park: "It is divided into five eras (chapters), many periods (pages), and epochs (paragraphs)" (Maxwell, 1968). That's true. But the eco-

Era	Period[1]	Epoch[2]
GEOLOGICAL TIMESCALE REFERENCED IN THIS BOOK		
Cenozoic 65.5 million years ago to the present	Quaternary 2.588 Ma to present	Holocene 11,700 years ago to present
		Pleistocene 2.588 mya to 11,700 years ago
	Neogene 23.03 Ma to 2.588 Ma	Pliocene 5.332 mya to 2.588 mya
		Miocene 23.03 mya to 5.332 mya
	Paleogene 65.5 Ma to 23.03 Ma	Oligocene 33.9 mya to 23.3 mya
		Eocene 55.8 mya to 33.9 mya
		Paleocene 65.5 mya to 55.8 mya
Mesozoic 251 million years ago to 65.5 million years ago	Cretaceous (K) 145.5 Ma to 65.5 Ma	Late K 99.6 mya to 65.5 mya
		Early K 145.5 mya to 99.6 mya
	Jurassic 199.6 Ma to 145.5 Ma	
	Triassic 251 Ma to 199.6 Ma	

[1] Time span in Ma (mega-annum).
[2] Time span in mya (millions of years ago).

systems—plants and animals, fungi and bacteria, the complex webs of life and death that make up our world—are the sentences and the meaning of the words.

Imagine, then, standing in one place amid the red rocks of the desert, the years racing backward at the rate of one a second. Days pass. The landscape flattens, greens, fills with blurs of animal and plant life. By the morning of the third day, warm waters are rolling in, advancing and retreating in waves, lapping higher every time. By the morning of the fifth day, you have traveled back to the Early Cretaceous and you are hundreds of feet underwater.

THE SHALLOW SEAS

At that point, 135 mya, the center of the North American continent is split by the Western Interior Seaway, a shallow sea that flows from the Arctic Ocean in the north to the Gulf of Mexico in the south, 3,000 miles, or 5,000 kilometers (km), long and about 1,200 miles (2,000 km) wide. East in the seaway is the island of Appalachia, still mysterious to this day; to the west lies the mountainous and geologically active island of Laramidia.

The land we call Big Bend lies south and east of Laramidia, well offshore. There are no ice caps to the north or south; the water level is hundreds of feet higher than our present level, reaching around 300 feet (90 meters) at its deepest. Big Bend is closer to the equator, and so the waters are warm and tropical, perhaps fueling vast hurricanes that pummel the distant shorelines. Plankton and foraminifera microfossils—as well as the remains of larger mollusks—paint a picture of a much saltier sea than those of the present.

These conditions are bad for corals. Instead, the reefs that carpet the sea bottom are beds of enormous rudist clams, bivalves that cluster with tangles of oysters and mollusks. Swimming above these reefs are clouds of fish and crustaceans, supporting a vast food web of everything from sharks to marine reptiles like long-necked plesiosaurs and whalelike, long-jawed pliosaurs.

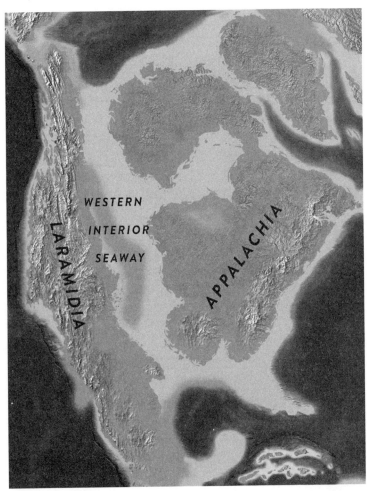

The North American continent 135 million years ago, when the Big Bend area was underwater in the southern end of the Western Interior Seaway.

For millions of years, the Western Interior Seaway rises and falls according to the pulse of tectonic movement and the climatic wobbles of the Earth. Some of the layers of sediment the seaway leaves behind will one day be visible on the high walls of the mighty Santa Elena and Boquillas Canyons and in the high cliffs of the Dead Horse Mountains and the Sierra del Carmen. But deep within the guts of the Laramidia, two vast tectonic plates are grinding together. The seafloor of the Western Interior Seaway has begun to lift, which will one day spell doom for the inland waterway. The ocean is beginning a slow retreat eastward.

By the time the Boquillas Formation is deposited (95–85 mya), the future park sits along Laramidia's continental shelf. Sediments of marine mud and limestone—composed of the shells of billions of plankton and microfossils—have accumulated on the sea bottom. The plesiosaurs have been replaced atop the food chain by mosasaurs like *Tylosaurus*, some of whose bones sink down into the ooze at the sea bottom to join the remains of fish, urchins, cephalopods, and vast numbers of shark teeth.

Run the clock forward a few millennia more and the waters have become shallower still. The seaway of the Pen Formation (85–82 mya) now resembles the clear, warm waters a few miles off a tropical shore. In this shallower environment, the sunny seas are patrolled by sharks, small mosasaurs like *Clidastes*, and fish like *Xiphactinus*, the gluttonous bulldog tarpon. Spiral-shelled ammonites and invertebrates of the marine shelf are also more common here.

THE BIG BEND DELTA

Time passes. Beneath the western edge of Laramidia, the dense Pacific Plate continues to slide beneath the lighter continental North American Plate, creating buckling tensions within the crust that force the continent's rock ever upward. The Interior Seaway makes its slow retreat toward the center of the North American Plate. In Big Bend, the water level drops, and drops, and drops.

As the seas retreat, a new ecosystem emerges in Big Bend, a complex mosaic of deltas, coastal seas, and estuarine swamps, bayous, and marshes. In this world of the Aguja Formation (83–72 mya) the line between the Interior Seaway and the coast is fluid, with sea levels rising and falling even as the ocean continues its overall retreat. In its place is a perfect environment for dinosaurs. The winding waterways are patrolled by shoals of fish and sharks, big turtles, and the great alligatoroid *Deinosuchus*. Herds of hadrosaurs graze and bellow along the shorelines, along with horned ceratopsids and armored nodosaurs. Tyrannosauroids stalk them from the forest shadows, while feathered dromaeosaurs pursue lizards and dinosaur hatchlings in the undergrowth.

The oceans, however, are not done with Big Bend just yet. They reappear in a geological instant to devour the deltas, pushing the shoreline and its dinosaurs back. A collection of sandstones, marine layers, and the remnants of beaches reveal a rise in sea levels. The sediments of the Pen Formation are still depositing on the western coast of the Western Interior Seaway. For a few thousand years, fish and crustaceans once again dominate the deposits of the Aguja.

Yet this late reappearance of the inland sea is only a short encore. By the appearance of the last deposited layer of the Aguja, the seas have once again retreated, this time for good. In their place lie the slow, murky waters of the delta and lake floodplains. Most of the dinosaurs are found in these fossiliferous upper shales.

Their return marks a transition; Big Bend is about to enter a new age of giants.

THE FLOODPLAIN OF GIANTS

We have now reached the Javelina Formation (72–67 mya), a period that records the full flowering of the Late Cretaceous. In Laramidia, the tectonic unrest beneath the continent has birthed the early Rocky Mountains, a chain of peaks running 3,000 miles (4,828 km) from modern British Columbia to West Texas, including the Mesa de Anguila west of Santa Elena Canyon and the Sierra del Carmen that extend into Mexico on the eastern border of the park. Big Bend now lies hundreds of feet above sea level. The seas and their coastal deltas are, in human terms, an impossibly distant memory.

The ground in Big Bend buckles downward, forming broad river basins filled with slow, winding rivers like those of the modern Brazos. When they overtop their banks, they deposit fresh swaths of river sediment, nourishing vegetation and leaving behind mudstones and colorful paleosols (ancient soils) in layers of reds, grays, blacks, greens, and purples. The plains are a patchwork of forest and meadowlands, kept open by the movements of the enormous sauropod *Alamosaurus*. Ridge-snouted hadrosaurs and enormous frilled ceratopsians live here too, as do tyrannosauroids and the immense pterosaur *Quetzalcoatlus*, one of the last and largest of its kind. The waterways are filled with fish, rays, and amphibians, and early carnivorous mammals creep about in the brush.

In the maroon mud soils laid down in the early Black Peaks Formation (67–66 mya), the remains of flowering plants, conifers, gar, and rays, as well as the bones of *Alamosaurus*, are fossilized. This formation is named for the three small black peaks that can be seen to the east of the Fossil Discovery Exhibit, on a 4-mile (6-km) round-trip hike on the Tornillo Flat.

Those sediments date to the precise geological moment when the dinosaurs disappear. Far to the south, an asteroid 10 miles (16 km) wide appears out of nowhere and smashes into the shallow waters of the Gulf of Mexico, striking with the force of 10 billion Hiroshima bombs. The impact is enough to liquefy the rock beneath the asteroid, blasting water and liquid rock into the stratosphere. As it returns to Earth, the liquid rock is deposited as a new set of mountains in the center of the crater called a peak ring.

The effects of the impact ripple out with murderous inevitability. When Dr. Sean Gulick and colleagues analyzed core samples from the peak ring in 2016, they found that minutes after the impact, crippling earthquakes and tsunamis as high as 1,640 feet

(500 meters) raged throughout the region. During the immediate aftermath, some floods run as far up the continental shelf as College Station, Texas. Hours after the impact, burning ejecta plummet down across the globe, spreading immense wildfires. Within days, clouds of burning debris are released into the atmosphere, including gigatons (a unit of 1 billion metric tons) of carbon and sulfur.

After the initial pulse of killing heat, a cold shroud settles over the world. The sun is blotted out. Photosynthesis stops for perhaps as long as 30 years, killing off plants first, then herbivores and carnivores, crashing food webs on land and at sea. Slowly, agonizingly, every land animal over 60 pounds, or 25 kilograms (kg), dies. Seventy percent of life on land, including all nonbird dinosaurs and pterosaurs, perishes along with 90 percent of ocean life, including the great mosasaurs and the spiral-shelled ammonites. Called the Cretaceous-Paleogene (K-Pg) extinction event and occurring around 66 mya, this was the worst disaster since the Permian extinction 185 million years earlier, when 90 percent of all life was killed off.

Although other parts of the world preserve the actual layer of the impact fallout (called the Cretaceous-Paleogene iridium layer), Big Bend seemingly does not. One moment, the nonbird dinosaurs are there in the layers of rock, and then they are gone forever.

THE HOTHOUSE FORESTS

We have now crashed into the Paleocene, the beginning of the Paleogene Period. The extinction of the dinosaurs and the ruination of Earth's global ecosystem have taken only a few seconds; at the rate we're moving, you could have blinked and missed it. At first glance, what sprouts back in the Paleogene Black Peaks Formation (66–56 mya) looks like the ecosystem that was there before the extinction event. Huge trees line sandy river channels and are preserved in petrified logjams of conifers. The lack of growth rings in these trees shows an environment of constant temperatures and no seasons. In these forests, mammals and birds are diversifying and exploiting newly opened niches that used to belong to non-bird dinosaurs.

Globally, the Earth is in an age of volcanoes. Eruptions lasting millennia dump carbon into the atmosphere at a rate similar to that of human industry today, causing global temperatures to spike 41–46°F (5–8°C) above average. Around 56 mya, the Earth enters a brutal hothouse period called the Paleocene-Eocene Thermal Maximum. Oceans rise and become more acidic, wiping out large swaths of animals that survived the Cretaceous extinction. Alligators and strange mammals live in warm polar jungles under the midnight sun. Far to the east of Big Bend, the dying seaway makes one last surge into the interior of the North American continent, before withdrawing into the Gulf of Mexico. In the west, the Rocky Mountains continue their rise, elevating Big Bend ever higher.

The growing slopes convert slow, meandering waterways into the faster, deeper rivers and forested swamps of the Hannold Hill Formation (56–50 mya), a mostly eroded deposit that is found only in a small northeastern section of the park and around the Fossil Discovery Exhibit. This formation's fauna is made up of early horse relatives like *Hyracotherium* and the hippolike *Coryphodon*, as well as the bearish *Titanoides* and assorted alligators, turtles, and snakes.

Beneath their feet, meanwhile, the Earth is waking up.

THE VOLCANIC AGE

By the mid-Eocene, the buildup of the Rocky Mountains, called the Laramide Orogeny, has reached Big Bend. Forces within the Earth's crust elevate the region several thousand feet above sea level. The merciless processes of erosion have gone to work on the Aguja, Javelina, and Hannold Hill Formations, wiping great stretches of them away. Atop these rocks, the Canoe Formation

(47.8–38 mya) is deposited in layers of sand and pebbles by tumbling, rapid-filled rivers. The spires and hoodoos of this formation are visible today on the western side of the road at the Fossil Discovery Exhibit.

Big Bend is now rocked by short periods of active volcanism mixed with intervals of relative quiet lasting a thousand to a million years. Some of the eruptions are large enough to dwarf the 1980 Mount St. Helens eruption in Washington, which the landscape has come to resemble. Magma bubbles into faults and underground fractures in the ground. As it hardens, it leaves behind injections of dense igneous rock that are slowly revealed by erosion. The forests of this turbulent world feature the brontothere *Megacerops* (which resembles a rhinoceros) and early carnivoran mammals like the fossa-shaped *Miocyon*.

At around the same time, the Chisos Formation (46–40 mya) records vast spills of lava across the landscape in places like the Lower Burro Mesa Pour-Off Trail and deep drifts of volcanic ash at Tuff Canyon. The eruptions and volcanic activity throw up the Chisos Mountains, 40 square miles of mountain range born of a super volcanic eruption. Even in periods of relative quiet, magma accumulates beneath the hills, cooling into laccoliths, uplifts, dikes, and sills that today dot the broken landscape. Although both formations are within the park, the best fossil discoveries occur in the Devil's Graveyard Formation (40–37 mya), outside park borders. As they all represent the same broader ecosystem, we have included all three.

By the Miocene Epoch (23–5 mya)—the beginning of the Neogene Period—the worst of the volcanism has quieted down. The Rocky Mountains have reached their final shape, leaving a landscape of high peaks and buckled valleys across the western part of the continent. The climate is beginning to dry and become cooler. Seasons take shape. Ice forms at the poles. The forests begin to die out as grasslands become dominant and spread across the now familiar landscapes of the park. In Big Bend, the sediments of the Delaho Formation (24–16 mya) and the Banta Shut-In Formation (10.3–4.9 mya) preserve grazing herds of the small rhinoceros *Menoceras*, the camel relative *Hypsiops*, bone-crushing dogs like *Epicyon*, and the saber-toothed cat *Nimravides*.

The volcanism has quieted, but the Earth isn't done moving. The birth of the Rocky Mountains has stretched out the North American Plate, creating deep north-to-south cracks. Seventeen million years ago, these cracks widen and crumble in great blocks, creating broad basins between two steep, high-cliffed ranges. This geographic region—which extends throughout most of the western United States—is called the Basin and Range Province. The Chisos Mountains sit within such a basin, first called the Sunken Block by Johan Udden in 1909, a term used for this area ever since. The ranges on either side of this basin are the Sierra del Carmen to the east and the Mesa de Anguila to the west near Santa Elena Canyon. As a result of the collapse, the limestone layer in the basin and the layer at the top of these ranges are the same age.

About 3 mya, during the Pliocene, the Rio Grande begins to flow from the San Juan Mountains of Colorado south into Lake Cabeza de Vaca in New Mexico. A million years later, large-scale cracks in the North American Plate are filled in by volcanic lava flows, redirecting the river of 1,896 miles (3,051 km) eastward to empty into the Gulf of Mexico. The modern landmarks of Big Bend—the mountains, the canyons, and the river course that gives the park its name—have all now taken shape.

ICE AGE PLAINS, DRYING DESERTS

We are now in the Pleistocene Epoch (2.5 mya to 11,700 years ago). In geological terms, we have practically reached the present. The cooling trend that began in the Miocene has advanced, and great walls of crushing glacial ice have rolled down from the north, dropping sea levels across the globe and creating a colder, drier world. Big Bend is spared a freeze during the last glacial advance, but as the climate fluctuates through periods of relative warmth and bitter cold, the river systems within the Big Bend region endure periods of long-term drought mixed with violent flooding. According to the collection of plant and animal remains in pack-rat middens, evergreen woodlands and pastures spread from the heights of the Chisos Mountains into the lowlands of the Tornillo Flat, nourished by mild winters, cool summers, and quite a bit of rain.

In these forests and meadows are animals we recognize today: mountain lions, black bears, and deer. They are joined by the last of the American megafauna: Columbian mammoths, American horses, and saber-toothed cats. On the cliffs of the Chisos Mountains, great condors ride the thermals, scanning for carrion.

By 20,000 years ago, the first humans have arrived in the Americas. The Earth is entering the interglacial period, a time of relative warmth that begins 11,000 years ago as the glaciers retreat. In Big Bend, the disappearance of those distant glaciers further dries the climate. The mammoths and saber-toothed cats vanish. The evergreen forests shrink back up the slopes of the Chisos Mountains, where their last remnants persist today. They are replaced first by scrubby grasslands, then by the spreading Chihuahuan Desert.

By around 4,000 years ago, Big Bend as we know it has taken shape. It is a landscape now defined by its dryness, save for the green oases of the high Chisos Mountains and the riparian corridor along the Rio Grande. Mountain lions stalk deer in arroyos of banded Cretaceous stone; in Santa Elena Canyon, lizards run across limestone beds and posture on seashells from that long-distant ocean. The years pass like years, not seconds. Visitors to the park now walk across the surface of unimaginably old rocks, and nobody can be sure what the next several millennia will bring.

⋅⋖ *3* ⋗⋅

MARINE BIG BEND

The BOQUILLAS and PEN FORMATIONS

BOQUILLAS FORMATION
Late Cretaceous
  from 95 Ma (Cenomanian Age) to 85 Ma (Santonian Age)
Time Traveler's Field Notes: *88 mya, March 30, 3:00 pm*
Western Interior Seaway

Y OU ARE FLOATING IN THE WARM WATERS, LITTLE WAVES LAP-
ping at your body. It's hot and sunny, the humid air heavy
on your face. As the waters close over your head, you drift down
toward the deep clays and silts of the seabed.

The bottom here is a gentle slope, more than a hundred feet
deep. The tangled mountains of corals you are used to in modern reefs are absent. Instead, the dim waters of the floor are covered with huge clamlike bivalves of the genus *Inoceramus*, some
of them three feet wide and six feet long. Their shells—encrusted
with smaller mollusks and wisps of algae—are open, the animal inside sieving the water for bits of plankton. Although the beds do
not offer the nooks and crannies of a coral reef, they are swarming

with life. Tiny fish and crustaceans school around them, darting inside the open shells whenever a shadow passes overhead. Sponges cluster and build soft superstructures around the great clams. Sea urchins and heart urchins make their spiny, blind way around and over the towering mollusks, and crinoids waft feathery arms like the petals of underwater flowers.

Here and there, the barnacle-encrusted bones of reptiles poke from beneath the ooze, boneworms boring away in search of flesh. When you dig your fingers into the warm muck and feel around, you pluck up a large shark's tooth. Close your eyes and listen, and you will hear a chorus of pops, wheezes, whoops, and grunts as the reef fish jostle and speak to one another. Brilliantly colored ammonites—looking like squids in coiled shells—float high above in the water column, or creep along the reefs, tentacles questing for prey. The whole landscape is a riot of constant motion—the darting, flashing movements of shoals of fish, the lazy glide of sharks, sudden bursts and black jets from squid and ammonites. Beneath them is the steady, drifting pulse of the clams themselves, fleshy, threadlike tentacles drifting out in the warm water.

A huge shadow falls over the reef. Some of the clams snap shut, closing around tiny fish. A few of the sharks make themselves scarce; the reef schools keep dancing, unconcerned. You sink down along the clams, just in case. A torpedo-shaped marine reptile has come to call.

The visitor is a *Plesioplatecarpus*, a 17-foot (5-meter) mosasaur related to modern monitor lizards. She moves overhead with lazy sweeps of a long, crescent-fluked tail, her broad fins held at an angle to reduce drag. Normally this is an ambush predator, lurking in the depths and flashing out after sharks or smaller mosasaurs, but the reef fish here are too small to be worth chasing. She's not here to hunt.

With a flick of her tail, the *Plesioplatecarpus* dives down toward a stretch of open sediment. More clams snap shut as she nears the reef. Then sediment billows and hazes as she rubs against the seafloor, tail beating, scattering the fish. Like a modern whale, she has her own share of barnacles and parasites, and the clam reef makes a good scratching post. Before long, the murky water hides her almost entirely. Still, you can feel the vibrations in the sediment beneath you, and ripples and eddies in the water.

Eventually, the mosasaur is satisfied. As she rests on the bottom, small fish gather around her to pluck at parasites and nibble at the scratches left by the clams. You kick off and slowly begin to rise up through the warm waters, away from the mudstones that will one day create the Boquillas Formation of Big Bend, toward the surface and the boiling sun.

GEOLOGY OF THE BOQUILLAS FORMATION

The rocks of Big Bend preserve a period when the region was located at a junction between the Western Interior Seaway and the North Atlantic or Tethys basin. Over that time, water levels rose and fell, leaving behind complex layers of marine sediments and calcareous oozes, leading to exposures of everything from massive limestones to shales a few inches thick.

Deposited during the Late Cretaceous in modern-day West Texas, the Boquillas Formation was named for the town of Boquillas ("little flags") and for the flagstone outcrop of the former post office of Big Bend National Park. The formation preserves a relatively shallow open marine platform where rudists and other animals with shells used the dissolved carbonate in the seawater to make their skeletons. As the animals died, other organisms grew on top of the shells, and skeletons built up to create a reef. The formation is packed with fossils. The oldest portion of the formation, the Ernst Member, contains flagstone, layers of limestone that split into layers a third of an inch to almost 2 inches (1.5 cm) thick. These "flaggy" layers can be seen best at the Ernst Tinaja in the park. The limestone, siltstone, and calcareous clay came from the bottom layer of this marine platform.

The younger San Vicente Member contains chalk, the compressed remains of layers of single-celled shelled creatures like foraminifera and coccolithophores. Marly clay, shale, and chalk also come from the bottom layer of this carbonate platform.

WHERE TO SEE THE BOQUILLAS FORMATION

Look for thin layers of flagstone at Ernst Tinaja (rock water well), or at the Mesa de Anguila on the right side of Santa Elena Canyon. You can also see parts of this deposit on the Hot Springs Trail or the Dagger Flat Auto Trail.

FOSSIL REMAINS OF THE BOQUILLAS FORMATION
Ichnofossils

Five different types of fossil marine burrows have been found in the Boquillas Formation. Four of them come from marine sediments, including *Rhizocorallium* burrows from the deep ocean's abyssal plains. They were made by polychaete ("many bristles") worms, a very ancient family that still exists in volcanic hydrothermal vents in the deep ocean. These burrows were used to store the worms' droppings. *Thalassinoides* ("like seagrass") burrows are networks of interconnected horizontal and vertical branches, created by burrowing shrimp as a shelter. Somewhat similar were the common *Chondrites* burrows. These small, branching burrows, which resemble plant roots, still exist today, possibly made by nematode worms or as fecal storage. *Planolites* burrows were simple straight or gently curved feeding tubes for deposit feeders like marine worms.

Finally, *Gastrochaenolites* are the club-shaped borings found on bivalve shells made by mussels that were lithophagic ("stone eaters"), using a gland secretion to weaken and remove the shells so that they could devour the animal inside.

Sea Urchins

Sea urchins have existed on the floors of Earth's oceans for the past 450 million years. They have no eyes but are still able to see with light-sensitive molecules between their moving spines and the foot that they extend to move. As detritivores, they clean up the dead plants and animals on the seafloor and are preyed on by starfish, nautiluses, ammonites, and baculites.

Sixteen species of fossil shells have been found in Big Bend so far, including the remains of globe-shaped and heart-shaped urchins from Early and Late Cretaceous formations. The extinct *Leiotomaster bosei* resembled the spiny globe-shaped urchins of today.

Bivalve Mollusks

Bivalves ("two shells"), such as clams, oysters, and mussels, are organisms that live on or under the seabed. The most familiar of these is the clam family, which evolved in the Early Jurassic (200 mya) and has been a fixture in aquatic environments ever since. Multiple species, including file clams, tellin clams, pointed nut clams, jingles, arks, and cockles, were found in the Big Bend area, as well as multiple species of large *Inoceramus* clams.

Bivalves are also notable for making up most of the reef structures in marine Big Bend, particularly a family called rudists. The temperature of the continental sea was higher than today's temperatures, and the water was much saltier, conditions that proved fatal to most corals. Rudist bivalves dominated instead. They were shaped like boxes, tubes, or rings that ranged from about an inch (2.5 cm) to 3.3 feet (1 meter). One shell was attached to the seafloor while the other opened and closed during filter feeding. They were eaten by animals that could crush the shells, such as rays, sawfish, and shell-crushing sharks like *Ptychodus*. Rudist reefs spanned hundreds of miles around the continental shelves of the Cretaceous seaways.

Fossilized rudist bivalves. Rudists had one cylindrical valve and one flat valve, like a cap, on top. When the cap was open, the animal could feed on organisms it filtered from the seawater. In the chunk of reef shown in the top half of the photo, a cylinder-shaped valve is bundled with other rudists extending up from the base. A flat cap valve is visible on the left side of the bottom piece of reef.

Rudists began to decline about 2.5 million years before the end in the Cretaceous extinction, which finally finished them off. In the Big Bend area, they went extinct primarily due to the movement of the Western Interior Seaway eastward into the present-day Gulf of Mexico. Chunks of rudist reef fossils have also been found in the Del Carmen, Santa Elena, and Pen Formations.

Gastropods

Gastropods are snails and slugs that have lived on land, in seas, and in freshwaters for more than 500 million years. With no skeleton or bones, snails have a stomach with a few vital organs in a shell and a "foot" for locomotion. Slugs do not have a shell, so their stomach and organs are spread out in their foot. They also have a radula—a tongue structure with rows of tiny teeth that helps them to break off food and scrape rocks, as well as to bore holes into the shells of bivalves to eat the animal within. Gastropods have a diverse range of diets depending on their habitat. Carnivorous snails eat worms, slugs, and small fish; grazers eat plant material in and out of water; filter feeders strain the water for plankton and organic scraps that fall from above; and detritivores clean up dead plants and animals.

Gastropods have been found in many of the formations of Big Bend, with true whelks and moon snails among the more than 52 fossil snail species known from the park.

Cephalopods

A group of mollusks that includes octopus and squid is best represented in the Mesozoic fossil record by a spiral-shelled group called ammonites. Resembling the modern nautilus but more closely related to squid, ammonites are named after Ammon, an Egyptian god depicted with ram's horns. (Ammonite genus names often end in the Greek root -*ceras*, which means "horn.")

First appearing 409 mya, ammonites likely resembled modern cephalopods. They had tentacles, ate with the same beaklike mechanism as their relatives, and used ink sacs to evade predators. Their shells were complicated adaptations, each divided into chambers with thin walls called septa. The shell had to be the same density as the seawater to function as an effortless flotation device; when an ammonite wanted to move up or down, fast or slow, it changed the density of its shell through the osmosis of salt water and the regulation of oxygen, nitrogen, and carbon dioxide.

In the Jurassic, ammonites rarely exceeded 9 inches (23 cm) in diameter, but by the Late Cretaceous many grew to over 2 feet (61 cm) in diameter. As with the nautilus, females were larger than males. They ate fish, crustaceans, sea plants, zooplankton, and corals, and they scavenged dead things that floated down to the seafloor. With their well-developed vision, they were fast-moving carnivores in the open ocean and around the reefs and seafloor, before going extinct with the dinosaurs at the end of the Cretaceous.

Baculites ("walking stick rock") were another type of cephalopod. Beginning as a tiny coil of one or two shell whorls or spirals, a baculite could grow from about 2.8 inches (7 cm) to 6.7 feet (2 meters). They inhabited the middle part of the water column. Males were one-third the size of the females. They had the same diet as the ammonites.

Both families make great index fossils because they are easy to identify, they evolved rapidly into new species, they had large populations for a very short time period, and they were found in marine sediments all over the world. Paleontologists use zones named for ammonite species to identify periods of time. The *Collignoniceras woolgari* Zone in the Boquillas Formation, for example, helped identify the mosasaurs of Big Bend as the oldest currently known in North America. More than 50 species of fossilized ammonites have been found in the Big Bend area.

Soft-bodied cephalopods rarely fossilize, and generally they only leave behind shells. In 2005, however, Lamar University paleontologists Dee Ann and Roger Cooper made a rare and incredible find: two soft-bodied squid fossils in the Boquillas Formation. The detailed carbon fossils were less than 2 inches (5 cm) long. The complete squid was shown, including the mantle body and fins along with tiny tentacles.

Fishes and Sharks

Cretaceous oceans, like those today, were filled with fishes and sharks. The Boquillas Formation preserves various indeterminate bony fishes, including the ray-finned fish *Laminospondylus transversus*, an extinct type of ladyfish resembling the modern skipjacks that inhabit highly salty deltas or lagoons. Shark teeth are also known from the formation, including the sharp teeth of *Cretalamna*, a relative of the enormous *Megalodon*.

Mosasaurs

Mosasaurs ("lizards from the Meuse River") were large, ocean-going reptiles related to lizards and snakes. They were enormous monitor lizards with paddles instead of claws. Mosasaurs descended from *Aigialosaurus*, a primitive monitor, a little over a yard long (1.1 meters), that hunted in water but likely slept and nested on land. The family eventually came to inhabit water full-time, their bodies becoming longer and more streamlined. Their limb bones reduced in length, and webbing between the long finger and toe bones gradually evolved into powerful paddles. Eventually, some mosasaurs developed a powerful, sharklike fluked tail that propelled them through the water. After the extinction of marine reptiles like plesiosaurs, pliosaurs, and ichthyosaurs, mosasaurs took over the niches of other large predators in global oceans during the Late Cretaceous, diversifying into multiple families, including the Tylosaurines (represented by the massive *Tylosaurus*) and the Mosasaurines (animals like the relatively small *Clidastes* and the massive, late-surviving *Mosasaurus*).

Mosasaurs were well adapted to thrive in Cretaceous seas. The family was notable for a double-hinged jaw able to open wide enough to swallow prey whole, like a modern snake. Recurved teeth pointed toward the back of the mouth and hooked the prey in place, while a set of pterygoid (palate) teeth in front of the throat helped pull the prey down the throat. Mosasaurs likely had sharp vision and an endothermic metabolism that kept their body temperature warmer than that of the water. Unlike many of their terrestrial relatives, mosasaurs gave birth to live young, using a strategy called ovoviviparity. Females incubated and hatched eggs inside their bodies and gave birth to live young. (Some modern snakes also do this.) Studies of the melanosomes, or pigments from fossilized mosasaur skin, suggest that many had dark-colored backs and lighter-colored bellies, similar to a great white shark or sperm whale.

Mosasaurs were large predators, able to hunt and devour many of the animals in the seas. Mosasaur coprolites—or fossilized dung—show ammonite shell fragments, and a mosasaur tooth embedded in a *Pachydiscus* ammonite shell suggests that ammonites were a common prey item. One fossilized mosasaur preserves the remains of a smaller mosasaur in its digestive tract, so a tendency toward cannibalism is evident.

Most of the mosasaur fossils known from Big Bend come from the Ernst Member, the oldest strata of the Boquillas. The animals are represented by skull and jaw fragments along with teeth, many of which have yet to be positively identified. Nonetheless, animals like *Tylosaurus*, *Plesioplatecarpus*, and *Clidastes* are known from similarly aged deposits in other parts of the former inland sea, and so they likely lived in Big Bend as well.

Notable Species of the Boquillas Formation

Inoceramus
(in-Nah-ser-a-mus)
("strong pot")
Order Pteriida
Family Inoceramidae
Part of a group of very large clams. *Inoceramus* had thick shells with prominent growth lines on the outside (like tree rings) and mother-of-pearl interiors. Their extreme size may have been a

product of the need for larger gills, an adaptation for the murky, oxygen-deficient waters at the bottom of the inland seas.

SIZE Up to 6.7 feet (2 meters) long and 3 feet (1 meter) wide.

FOSSIL HISTORY Originally named in 1814 by English naturalist James Sowerby, *Inoceramus* fossils are found worldwide and are common index fossils for distinguishing different ages in the later Mesozoic. Nineteen species of *Inoceramus* are known from the Boquillas Formation; they are the most common marine fossils found from the Late Cretaceous in the Big Bend area.

BIG BEND FOSSILS Complete and incomplete shells, some of remarkable size. Very large pearls have been reported pressed within the fossilized shells.

DIET Filter feeder. Plankton and other nutrients sifted from the seawater.

NATURAL HISTORY *Inoceramus* lived in the nutrient-rich waters near the shore of the Western Interior Seaway and provided shelter to small fish and eels. It was the prey of shell-crushing sharks like *Ptychodus* and rays of all sizes, including sawfish. It used a large foot to move its body around to find better places to feed.

Allocrioceras
(Al-low-Kree-oh-Sair-as)
("different ram horn")
Order Ammonitida
Family Anisoceratidae

A small and distinctive ammonite, with a fully ribbed and widely coiled shell that resembles a ram's horn. The distinctive shell makes it easy to recognize, and thus it is a perfect index fossil for dating specific deposits.

SIZE A bit larger than an American quarter.

FOSSIL HISTORY Originally named in 1926, the genus has been found in Colombia, the United States, Europe, and South Africa.

BIG BEND FOSSILS *Allocrioceras hazzardi* was a common species during the Turonian Age (88 mya) of the Late Cretaceous. Its remains have helped date an index fossil zone found between the Ernst Member, the oldest Boquillas strata, and the San Vicente, the youngest.

DIET Carnivore. Crinoids—ancient sea lilies—and small fish.

NATURAL HISTORY *Allocrioceras* was an open-ocean organism, floating in the water column with its head oriented upward, like that of a nautilus. It was unusually small compared with most adult ammonites and may have been devoured by specialist shell-crushers or mosasaurs.

Paralbula
(Par-ah-Al-Byu-lah)
("near whitish")
Order Albuliformes
Family Albulidae

A genus of ray-finned bonefish ancestral to today's bonefish. Instead of individual teeth, these fish have small plates of up to an inch (2.5 cm) wide with teeth that look like flattened spheres about ⅛ of an inch (2–3 mm) in length. Each crown has radiating ridges from the center, like a drawing of a sun's rays. As teeth wear away, new spheres rise up out of the plate like bubbles from boiling water.

SIZE Up to 41 inches (105 cm) long, with a weight of up to 14 pounds (6.4 kg).

FOSSIL HISTORY The genus was originally described in 1940. The species name *P. casei* means "Case's near whitish, referring to paleontologist Gerard R. Case; and *P. marylandica* ("near whitish of Maryland") is named for the original discovery site.

BIG BEND FOSSILS Primarily known for its distinctive teeth.

DIET Shell-eating carnivore. Crustaceans, mollusks, fish eggs, and larvae, as well as worms from the seafloor.

NATURAL HISTORY Like their modern relatives, *Paralbula* may have followed the rays that used their winglike fins to stir up the seafloor and expose crabs and shrimp, on which they also fed. They possibly moved from tropical waters to shallow mud or sand flats to feed with the incoming tide. They likely spawned in the open sea and were the prey of larger fish, sharks, and mosasaurs. Modern bonefish can gulp air when their water is oxygen-poor; perhaps *Paralbula* could as well.

Ptychodus
(Ty-Koh-dus)
("folded teeth")
Clade Elasmobranchii
Family Ptychodontidae

A large shark adapted to feeding on shelled animals. Its teeth had horizontal ripples on their domed surfaces for better crushing of hard shells. *Ptychodus* had about 200 such folded teeth in each jaw, with up to 550 teeth per individual. A fossil tooth plate measured about 22 inches (55 cm) long by 18 inches (45 cm) wide. *Ptychodus* also had serrated spines on its back and likely grew to remarkable sizes.

SIZE Up to about 33 feet (10 meters) long.

FOSSIL HISTORY The first remains of *Ptychodus* were teeth found in England and Germany, in the first half of the eighteenth century. In 1868, Joseph Leidy, an American paleontologist, reported a broken tooth in Kansas, marking the first *Ptychodus* in North America. *Ptychodus mortoni* ("Morton's folded teeth") is the only species currently known from Big Bend.

BIG BEND FOSSILS Skulls, dorsal fin spines, and teeth.

DIET Shell-eating carnivore. Crustaceans, bivalves, rudists, and other animals secured to the reef or seafloor, as well as carrion.

NATURAL HISTORY *Ptychodus* likely frequented the deeper water around the seabed or reefs. Although fully grown individu-

Shell-crunching *Ptychodus* shark. Instead of competing for fish in deeper waters, these sharks found a niche feeding on mollusks in the shallows of the Western Interior Seaway.

als were likely too large for predators to tackle successfully, young *Ptychodus* may have been prey for mosasaurs, larger fish, and other species of shark.

Plesioplatecarpus
(Plee-see-oh-Plat-ee-Kar-pus)
("near flat wrist")
Order Squamata
Family Mosasauridae

A medium-sized mosasaur. Its body is short, with a tail twice the length of the body, complete with a two-lobed vertical tail fluke. The skull is notably shorter and flatter than that of other mosasaurs, with nostrils positioned forward but facing outward on its snout. It has about 20 teeth in each jaw, the lowest number of any known mosasaur. The name *Plesioplatecarpus* refers to its flat wrist bones, an adaptation that likely made its paddles more efficient and streamlined.

SIZE Somewhat small for a mosasaur. Adults reached around

16 feet (4.8–5 meters) long and weighed between 340 and 360 pounds (154–164 kg).

FOSSIL HISTORY The genus name *Plesioplatecarpus* was coined in 2011 by Takuya Konishi and Michael W. Caldwell to incorporate *Platecarpus planifrons*, which was found to be distinct from *Platecarpus* in the mosasaur family tree.

BIG BEND FOSSILS A complete skull with conical teeth, disarticulated skull fragments missing the snout, front limbs and shoulder fragments, numerous vertebrae, and a quadrate (the bone that holds the lower jaw to the skull).

DIET Carnivore. Cephalopods like ammonites, baculites, and squid, as well as fish, smaller mosasaurs, and sharks.

NATURAL HISTORY *Plesioplatecarpus* lived in the open sea and gave birth to live young. A swift and agile hunter itself, its relatively small size may have made it prime prey for larger sharks and mosasaurs, such as *Tylosaurus*.

Tylosaurus
(Tie-loh-sore-rus)
("knob lizard")
Order Squamata
Family Mosasauridae

A large mosasaur. It had a relatively short body and a long tail. The body was covered in diamond-shaped, snakelike scales that made it a hydrodynamically fast swimmer. Its jaws contained around 52 large, conical teeth, as well as 20–22 pterygoid (palate) teeth. Its long, cylindrical snout contained a toothless stretch of the jaw on the very front—a knob, which gives the species its name.

SIZE *Tylosaurus kansasensis* was about 16 feet (5 meters) long and weighed about 440 pounds (200 kg). *Tylosaurus nepaeolicus* was 23 feet (7 meters) long and weighed about 1,102 pounds (500 kg).

FOSSIL HISTORY Two species are known from Big Bend. The

first, *Tylosaurus kansasensis* ("from Kansas"), was named for the state in which it was found by Michael J. Everhart, a paleontologist notable for his research on the Cretaceous inland sea, collected in the book *Oceans of Kansas*. The larger and longer-snouted *Tylosaurus nepaeolicus* ("of the Solomon River") was collected by Benjamin Franklin Mudge in 1877 about half a mile from the Solomon River in Kansas. In 2007, paleontologists Gordon L. Bell Jr. and Kenneth R. Barnes reported that a *Tylosaurus nepaeolicus* found in the Big Bend area had three small *Platecarpus* mosasaurs in its fossilized stomach.

BIG BEND FOSSILS A complete skull, skull fragments, numerous vertebrae, front limbs and shoulder fragments, and conical teeth were found in the older San Vicente Member (89–85 mya) of Boquillas.

DIET Carnivore. Fish, smaller mosasaurs, sharks, and ammonites.

NATURAL HISTORY Likely the apex predator of the seas in which it lived, *Tylosaurus* lived primarily in the open ocean, competing for prey with large sharks like *Cretoxyrhina* that resembled the great white. Several *Tylosaurus* fossils have been found with healed wounds and broken bones inflicted by other mosasaurs, whether in territorial disputes or during mating. The toothless knob may have been used to ram other mosasaurs.

PEN FORMATION
Late Cretaceous
from 85 Ma (Santonian Age) to 82 Ma (Early Campanian Age)
Time Traveler's Field Notes: *84 mya, July 2, 8:00 pm*
Western Interior Seaway

IT HAS BEEN A GRAY EVENING, A HAZE ROLLING IN LIKE FOG FROM the west. The sunset was a shower of fire and gold, sparking off the particulates thrown into the air. Somewhere far away in Mexico, a mountain is erupting, spewing carbon and gas into the sky. It is a minor eruption, as these things go—not enough to drop the temperatures of the planet—but the farthest impacts of the ash cloud are felt even here, out on the Interior Seaway. Soon, the infusion of iron sulfides will nourish blooms of phytoplankton, pumping nutrients into the food chain.

As you dive, the ocean sparks to life around you. The water column is filled with bioluminescent plankton, flashing in streaks of blue and green as you swim. Below, ammonites jet resentfully away from your kicking legs, before returning to inspect the flotsam at the surface of the water. A great shift change is occurring all around you; deep-water species are creeping into the shallows, lured out of their haunts by the vanishing light. They rise in alien flickers out of the dark, the faint pulsing glow of jellyfish and the fast flashing of squid, journeying up from the depths to hunt for prey. They leave trails as they disturb the plankton, colorful smears that flash and slowly die in the gloom.

There are other hunters abroad tonight. A swift *Squalicorax*—resembling a modern mako shark—zips past you, colored water streaming like contrails in its wake. Specialized pits on its snout help it detect movement in the water. You keep still, but it is after other prey tonight. It tracks the flashes in the dark, flicks its tail, and darts forward, jaws slinging forward to snap up an unwary squid. And then it's gone into the dark.

Around you bits of ash are dissolving in the water, spinning down, down, down, toward the oyster beds below. Far from the blast zone, these coastal waters are merely receiving a taste of some distant eruption. It is your first brief experience with volcanism in the region that will one day be Big Bend. It will not be the last.

GEOLOGY OF THE PEN FORMATION

The Pen Formation's name comes from the Chisos Pen, an old camping and branding site north of the Chisos Mountains. The Pen Formation is primarily dark bluish-gray mudstone, mixed with marl, a clay that weathers a yellowish gray. The chalky limestone and calcareous sandstone sediments were laid down by a regressing sea, and the marl suggests shallow water. The clay in this formation contains bentonite, which is created the moment volcanic ash containing glass crystals falls into water, marine or fresh, turning the glass into clay with a waxy, soapy texture. Their presence suggests that volcanic activity—and the mountain building in western Laramidia—was heating up.

The Pen Formation also contains sediments from a brief transgression, or a time when water came farther on land during the deposition of the Aguja Formation. Called the McKinney Springs Tongue, a dark gray thin shale represents an ancient seacoast that was deposited between the Rattlesnake Mountain sandstone and the Terlingua Creek sandstone members of the Aguja Formation.

WHERE TO SEE THE PEN FORMATION

Head to McKinney Springs along Ore Flat Road or check out rock deposits in the Maverick or Mariscal Mountains.

FOSSIL REMAINS OF THE MARINE PEN FORMATION
Sea Urchins

Hemiaster texanus was an extinct species of heart urchin, a family that still exists in modern seas and oceans. The elongated, heart-shaped animals had closely crowded spines, which contained cilia that helped them move, breathe, feed, and burrow in the sand or mud. As detritivores, they ate organic matter in and on the seafloor.

Bivalve Mollusks

The rudist reefs from the Boquillas Formation continued into the Pen Formation, including animals like *Inoceramus*. New species of rudists, such as the cone-shaped *Durania terlinguae* ("rotary of Terlingua"), appeared as well.

Rudists were joined by sprawling beds of oysters that thrived in the extremely salty waters of the Pen Formation. Species included *Exogyra ponderosa* ("outside circle from massive turns"), an extinct relative of modern honeycomb oysters, and *Pseudoperna congesta* ("congested or overpopulated false leg"), extinct tiny true oysters that clustered on giant *Inoceramus* clams. Some of these fossils show signs of predation by fossil borer worms, which bored through their shells to devour the soft animal within.

Cephalopods

Ammonites remained common in the shallower seas on the Pen Formation. They include species like the index fossil *Texanites texanus* ("Texan Texan thing"), which lived during the Santonian Age (86–83 Ma) of the Late Cretaceous. Larger ammonites appeared as well. *Placenticeras* are known from opalized mother-of-pearl shells measuring 3.3 feet (1 meter) in diameter. *Placenticeras whitfieldi* is found only in the Pen Formation, but *P. meeki*, *P. intercalare*, *P. syrtale*, and *P. placenta* survived into the Aguja Formation.

Eutrephoceras dekayi, a nautilus with a nearly round conchlike shell, and *Baculites ovatus*, a straight-shell ammonite, are also found in these deposits.

Fishes and Sharks

Fish remains from this deposit are largely limited to teeth and scattered parts, especially from big predators like the bulldog tarpon *Xiphactinus*, the goblinlike shark *Scapanorhynchus*, and garfish.

Mosasaurs

These sea reptiles continued to dominate the Pen Formation seas. As the waters grew shallower, however, giant oceangoing predators like *Tylosaurus* became less common, their place taken by small mosasaurs like *Clidastes* and the somewhat larger *Ectenosaurus*.

Notable Species of the Marine Pen Formation

Xiphactinus
(Zye-Fak-tih-nus)
("sword ray")
Order Ichthyodectiformes
Family Ichthyodectidae

An enormous ray-finned fish, resembling a modern tarpon. Its fins were made of either bony or soft spines covered with webs of skin, like those of modern tuna and swordfish. Its lower jaw jutted out and up, giving it the nickname "bulldog tarpon." Its fangs measured up to 4 inches long.

SIZE Adults up to 20 feet (4–6 meters) long, weighing up to 1,000 pounds (226–454 kg).

FOSSIL HISTORY Originally discovered by Joseph Leidy in the Kansas chalk in 1870, and subsequently known from multiple dramatic finds in the chalk layers of the former inland sea.

BIG BEND FOSSILS Skull, jaw fragments, and vertebrae. Many of these were collected during the WPA quarry work in 1938–1939. The *Xiphactinus* remains uncovered in the region are not clear enough to identify to the species level.

DIET Carnivore. Fish, smaller sharks, and young mosasaurs.

NATURAL HISTORY *Xiphactinus* likely filled the same niche as

Xiphactinus, the bulldog tarpon. As big as a full-sized car, this fish had a prominent jaw, and fangs that were the width of a human hand.

living swordfish and large sharks, that of a fast, adaptable, and indiscriminate predator. The genus has a reputation for having eyes bigger than its stomach, based on the discovery of the remains of a 13-foot (3.9-meter) *Xiphactinus* that died in the act of swallowing a 6-foot (1.8-meter) *Gillicus arcuatus*, a related fish.

Cretalamna
(Krete-ah-Lamb-nah)
("chalk shark")
Order Lamniformes
Family Otodontidae

A medium-sized, heavily built shark with a torpedo-shaped body. It had a pointed snout filled with large sharp teeth, a tall dorsal fin, and a crescent-shaped tail fluke. It is an ancestor of the extinct giant *Otodus megalodon*.

SIZE Up to 9.8 feet (2–3 meters) long.

FOSSIL HISTORY Originally named by Louis Agassiz in 1835, the genus rapidly became a wastebasket for unrelated shark fossils. Subsequent research has shown it to contain species from North Africa as well as North America, where the primary species is *Cretalamna appendiculata* ("chalk shark with thick tooth roots"). This is the species known from Big Bend.

BIG BEND FOSSILS Known only from triangular teeth with a large razor-sharp cusp (tooth point) and a tiny sharp cusplet (smaller tooth point) on each side.

DIET Carnivore. Fish, young marine reptiles, pterosaurs, sea turtles, oceanic birds, and squid.

NATURAL HISTORY An adaptable, generalist carnivore, *Cretalamna* was likely capable of surviving in a vast array of marine habitats, from the open ocean to shallower waters. It may have been a prey item for large mosasaurs. Some researchers have suggested that the species declined due to increased competition with newer generalist sharks and the withdrawal of the Western Interior Seaway from the Big Bend area.

Squalicorax
(Skwa-lih-Core-ax)
("crow shark")
Order Lamniformes
Family Anacoracidae

A medium-sized shark. On the crescent-shaped tail fluke, the top lobe is longer than the bottom lobe. In life, it likely resembled a modern gray reef shark. Among Mesozoic sharks, it is the only one known to have serrated teeth.

Squalicorax, the crow shark. Named for its presumed habit of scavenging, this was the only shark in the Mesozoic that had serrated teeth.

SIZE Up to 16 feet (2–5 meters) long, weighing between 500 and 1,000 pounds (227–454 kg).

FOSSIL HISTORY Named by paleontologist Louis Agassiz in 1843 and subsequently found throughout the American interior. Species found in Big Bend were *Squalicorax kaupi*, *S. pristodontus*, *S. yangaensis*, and *S. lindstomi*.

BIG BEND FOSSILS Known only from small serrated triangular teeth.

DIET Generalist carnivore. Fish, small mosasaurs, cephalopods, birds, and carrion.

NATURAL HISTORY One of the most common marine predators of the Western Interior Seaway, where it may have snatched pterosaurs bobbing in the water or out of the air. Likely preyed upon by larger sharks, *Xiphactinus*, and mosasaurs.

Cretorectolobus olsoni
(Creh-Toh-rekt-Toh-loh-bus)
("Olson's Cretaceous carpet shark")
Order Lamniformes
Family Orectolobidae

A large carpet shark. Its family is currently known as wobbegongs, an Australian Aboriginal name meaning "shaggy beard," referring to the barbels, or whiskers, around its mouth. This flat shark had two rows of fanglike teeth around the upper jaw and a lower jaw with three or four rows of spiky teeth.

SIZE An average length of about 4 feet (1.25 meters), but some have been found to measure up to 10 feet (3 meters).

FOSSIL HISTORY *Cretorectolobus olsoni* was named by Gerald R. Case in 1978 from North American deposits, though other species of the genus are also known from the United Kingdom.

BIG BEND FOSSILS All are known from teeth and teeth fragments.

DIET Carnivore. Fish around the reefs, smaller sharks, octopus, and squid.

NATURAL HISTORY Modern wobbegongs dwell on the sea bottom, where their colorful camouflage renders them invisible to both predators and prey. Their barbels have electrosensory receptors to feel the movement and heartbeat of prey. Present-day wobbegongs hold larger prey until it dies before devouring it in chunks. Perhaps *Cretorectolobus* did so as well.

Ischyrhiza
(Is-kee-Riz-ah)
("strong snout")
Order Rajiformes
Family Rajidae

A large sawfish ray with a flattened head and body and large pectoral fins fused to the body like wings. The remainder of the body resembled a shark, with two large dorsal fins. The long, flat sawfish snout, or rostrum, made up 15–25 percent of the length of its body. The snout had 14–37 teeth or rostral spines projecting from either side. This rostrum held electroreceptor organs that helped it detect the heartbeat and muscular movement of nearby prey.

SIZE A little over 3 feet (1 meter) long.

FOSSIL HISTORY Originally described by Joseph Leidy in 1856. The rostral spines are the most common remains from this ancient sawfish. *Ischyrhiza mira* and *I. avonicola* were the most common species of sawfish rays found in the Pen Formation.

BIG BEND FOSSILS Teeth, denticles, and rostral spines.

DIET Shell-eating carnivore. Fish, crustaceans, and bivalves.

NATURAL HISTORY Like modern sawfish, *Ischyrhiza* likely swung its snout from side to side to unearth and trap shelled creatures, slash through schools of fish, and defend itself in combat with predators or rival males. Its tiny teeth grew close together, forming a pavement in the mouth, used to crush mollusk shells. *Ischyrhiza* may have traveled in schools in the ancient delta and estuaries, migrating like salmon to freshwater breeding grounds. Today, sawfish are considered to be critically endangered.

Clidastes
(klih-Das-tees)
("locked vertebrate")
Order Squamata
Family Mosasauridae

A small, generalist mosasaur. With a long slim torso, a narrow rib cage, and a short tail, it was a streamlined, fast swimmer. When viewed from above, the snout is narrow and triangular, with forward-facing eyes. There are between 28 and 36 teeth on each jaw, and the pterygoid teeth in the back of the palate aid in swallowing prey whole. The smallest mosasaur fossil found so far in the Big Bend region is a *Clidastes*.

SIZE Up to 20 feet (2–6 meters) long.

FOSSIL HISTORY Discovered by Edward Drinker Cope in Alabama's Mooreville Chalk in 1869. The genus name *Clidastes* is derived from the interlocking heads of its backbone and tail vertebrae. The species name *liodontus* refers to the smooth nonserrated enamel on its sharp cone-shaped teeth. *Clidastes liodontus* ("locked vertebrae with smooth teeth") was the only mosasaur species of this genus found in the Big Bend area.

BIG BEND FOSSILS A complete skull with a cone-shaped snout, a complete frontal skull bone, neck (cervical) vertebrae, and a maxilla (upper jaw) with 15 positions for sharp conical teeth on each side.

DIET Carnivore. Primarily fish, turtles, and cephalopods.

NATURAL HISTORY Too small to compete with bigger deep-water mosasaurs, *Clidastes* likely frequented shallower parts of the Western Interior Seaway. A swift, shallow-water predator, it may have given birth to live young in secluded lagoons and estuaries. Young *Clidastes* were likely snapped up by large sharks and fish like *Xiphactinus*.

ᴖᴄᴄ *4* ᴐᴐᴖ

DINOSAUR FLOODPLAINS

The AGUJA, JAVELINA, and CRETACEOUS BLACK PEAKS FORMATIONS

AGUJA FORMATION
Late Cretaceous
from 83 Ma to 72 Ma (Campanian Age)
Time Traveler's Field Notes: 75 mya, December 25, 8:00 am
3 miles inland of the Western Interior Seaway

S UNRISE ON THE BAYOU. THE MORNING LIGHT COMES CREEP-
ing through the branches, falling through open patches of the
canopy. Blue shadows stretch between massive trunks. You're
standing on a game trail that leads up toward the water, the mud
soft beneath your boots, the air heavy with the smell of pollen, wet
earth, and decay, but there's a trace of salt on the breeze from the
nearby delta.

The vegetation here would not be entirely unfamiliar to a person visiting the Lower Rio Grande Valley. Palmettos and sabal

palms crowd between tall stands of cypress and flowering trees, dropping a dense cascade of dead leaves to the muddy ground. There is no dawn chorus of songbirds, though. Instead, clatters and hoots and chirrups filter through the trees, produced by frogs and toothed birds. Mosquitoes whine around you, searching for a meal of blood. You wave them away and begin to walk, following a path carved out of the forest by foraging dinosaurs.

Herbivores like the shovel-beaked hadrosaur *Aquilarhinus* have left ample signs of their presence. Even in the dim light, you can pick out the partially consumed rotting logs, saplings shouldered over and stripped, scrapes in the bark of the tall trees. Here and there you find broad, three-toed footprints in the mud, some of them filled with brown water and wriggling with tadpoles and mosquito spawn. Dragonflies flit by, plucking up biting insects.

You slow as the path leads down toward the lazy waters of the bayou. Side-necked turtles are hauling themselves out on half-sunken logs. The broad head of a large crocodilian breaches the surface—a young *Deinosuchus*, thirteen feet long and still growing rapidly. Soon he will be too large for the sluggish river and will head downstream into the brackish marshlands and lakes, to prey on sea turtles and grazing dinosaurs. For now, he's not hunting—but you keep well away from the water.

On the far bank, something is moving through the brush. A group of hadrosaurs emerges out of the shadows in near silence. The largest of them, a bull seventeen feet long with drooping wattles and a bright blue nasal crest, snorts as he catches wind of you. Even from where you're standing across the bayou, you can see that the bull moves with a slight limp, the product of some old injury. The others are a bit smaller and more dully colored. Their odor pervades the air, dry, with the stink of methane and musk.

Together the herd lingers at the water's edge, grunting softly. The big male is eyeing you and the *Deinosuchus* with equal distrust. Then, abruptly, he charges into the water, letting loose a bellowing roar. Turtles scramble and plop off their logs; the *Dei-nosuchus* jerks its head beneath the surface. Wavelets and ripples cross the tea-stained waters of the bayou. The big male swishes his tail and snorts again, dipping his head to drink. The others come down to the water to drink as well, hissing and grunting, heads bobbing up on occasion to check for danger. Several feet downstream, you see the *Deinosuchus* reappear, a silent shape in the water.

You walk on. It's going to be a beautiful day.

GEOLOGY OF THE AGUJA FORMATION

For millions of years, the Aguja Formation straddled the border between land and sea, with deposits from saltwater lagoons, coastal estuaries, deltas, forests, and marshes, a depositional environment resembling those of coastal Louisiana. Six different members are known for this formation. The oldest, the basal sandstone member, was a delta with a mix of fresh river water that poured into the seaway, represented by sandstones from beaches and high sea levels. The lower shale member shows a mix of shales from lower sea levels and lignite (primitive coal), a sign of freshwater swamps and marshes. Then came younger marine members, each composed of sandstones from their sea levels: the Rattlesnake Mountain sandstone, the McKinney Springs Tongue of the Pen Formation, and then the Terlingua Creek sandstone. For a few thousand years, fishes and crustaceans once again dominate the deposits.

Finally, the youngest layer, the upper shale member, preserves a slow-moving delta floodplain. Most of the dinosaur fossils found from the Late Cretaceous Period in Big Bend are known from this layer. By the appearance of the last deposited layer of the Aguja, the oceans have once again retreated, this time for good. In their place lie the slow, murky waters of the delta and lake floodplains.

In 1992, the paleontologists Timothy R. Rowe, Richard L.

Cifelli, Thomas M. Lehman, and Anne Weil wrote about the wealth of discoveries they had made near the town of Terlingua, revealing the inhabitants of an ancient estuary or bay in the Aguja Formation. They called this the Terlingua Local Fauna. These organisms would also have been found within the modern boundaries of the park.

WHERE TO SEE THE AGUJA FORMATION

Head out along the trail between the McKinney Springs and Roys Peak Vista campsites, or drive along Route 13 between Slickrock Mountain and Croton Peak. You can also look around the western Maverick entrance station at the Badlands wayside, or along River Road East around San Vicente Crossing.

FOSSIL REMAINS OF THE AGUJA FORMATION

Plants

The forests of the Aguja Formation would have somewhat resembled a cross between a tropical rain forest and an East Texas bayou, with tropical evergreens making up most of the canopy. Other plant species included *Agujoxylon olacaceae*, a flowering tree in the maple family with a canopy of between 131 feet and 164 feet (40-50 meters) high. Its maximum diameter was 4.3 feet (1.3 meters) with no tree rings, suggesting an environment that remained steadily warm and wet for extended periods with no seasonal changes for millions of years. Nineteen stumps are rooted in place in dark olive-gray mudstone.

Ichnofossils

Ophiomorpha ("snake shape") are near-shore burrows created by crustaceans like the modern ghost shrimp. The inside is relatively smooth, but the outside has small round fecal pellets packed into it to give the burrow support.

Mollusks and Gastropods

Shelled marine animals from the Pen Formation lingered through the middle of the Aguja Formation, including *Inoceramus* clams in the deeper deposits. New species of oysters also appeared, like *Flemingostrea subspatulata* ("Fleming's not quite a spatula oyster"). This extinct oyster had several large layers of shell on the top and bottom to make it difficult for predators to find the tasty morsel within the layers.

As the seaway moved eastward over the millennia, however, the community of marine shelled animals began to vanish from Big Bend.

Fishes and Sharks

The braided deltas, marshes, rivers, and lagoons of the Aguja Formation fostered a remarkable diversity of fishes, such as the formidable, long-snouted gar, much like the alligator gar found in Texas today.

The spiked hybodus ("hump-toothed") river sharks called *Lonchidion selachos* ("spear shark") patrolled the muddy waterways, and freshwater whiptail rays and skates devoured rudists and fish. Sawfish rays (for example, *Ischyrhiza texana*) and some sharks from the Pen Formation (such as *Cretorectolobus olsoni* and *Squalicorax*) lingered in the deeper marine environments of the Aguja Formation and are known from teeth or denticle fossils.

Amphibians

Frogs, toads, and salamanders have been identified through jaws and bones found in fossil form in the Aguja. Among them were *Albanerpeton nexuosum* ("white creeping swimmer"), an early relative of modern siren salamanders, with a thick, robust head and neck for burrowing, and small osteoderms in its skin. Although *Albanerpeton* inhabited land environments, it was tied to the water and went extinct as Big Bend became drier 72 mya. Hundreds of jaws and teeth have been found in the Terlingua Local Fauna of the Aguja.

Turtles

The bays and rivers of the Aguja sheltered numerous turtles, including large sea turtles like *Terlinguachelys* ("Terlingua turtle") in the Western Interior Seaway, along with the big side-necked turtles like *Chupacabrachelys* ("chupacabra turtle"). These are known from skeletal remains, including shells and shell plates.

Squamates

Squamates (scaled reptiles reptiles, such as lizards, snakes, and their relatives) are well known from this formation. The largest of them, the mosasaurs, remained a presence in the seas of the Aguja, but fossil evidence is too scrappy to assign it to known animals. On land, the brush and understory of the early Aguja coastal environment played host to the big predatory monitor *Dryadissector shilleri* ("Shiller's dissector of forest nymphs"), whose scalpel-sharp teeth are common enough to suggest it competed with small predatory theropod dinosaurs.

The later Terlingua estuaries sheltered animals like *Peneteius aquilonius*, the first known example of a lizard that had molars like an insectivore mammal, and *Odaxosaurus piger* ("lazy biting lizard"), a large burrowing beaded lizard known from teeth, jaw, and osteoderms. Also present was *Apsgnathus triptodon* ("backward jaw with worn teeth"), a new genus and species of extinct lizard with overlapping scales, along with whiptail lizards with long tails akin to those still common in the park today.

Snakes were also present in the Aguja, having evolved from lizards in the Early Cretaceous. *Coniophis presidens* ("early small snake"), a small, nonvenomous burrowing snake, is one of the most primitive members of its family currently known. Modern snakes have jaws that can unhinge to swallow large prey, but the large head of *Coniophis* resembled a lizard's, with hinged jaws and hooked teeth, meaning it likely preyed on smaller animals, such as salamanders and smaller reptiles.

Crocodilians

Moving through these estuarine environments were also enormous crocodiles, such as the alligator relative *Deinosuchus* ("terrible crocodile"), which preyed largely on turtles but also likely attacked and killed dinosaurs. Smaller species of crocodilians, such as *Goniopholis* ("angled scale"), are also known from freshwater deposits.

Dinosaurs

Easily the most famous of all extinct organisms, dinosaurs were a large, extremely diverse family of animals, ranging in size and shape from massive sauropods and horned ceratopsians to big predatory theropods and modern birds. The name "dinosaur" means "terrible lizard," but they actually belonged to the larger family of archosaurs, which includes crocodiles and birds. Dinosaurs evolved during the Triassic Period, around 240–230 mya. Their distinctive hips and limbs allowed them to move more efficiently than their competition—a flourishing population of crocodilian archosaurs—and they went on to dominate Mesozoic land ecosystems. One family of dinosaurs—birds—remains extremely successful today.

Dinosaurs are presently divided into two groups. The name of the Ornithischia ("birdlike hipped") branch is somewhat confusing. Although the animals in this lineage have pubic bones that point backward and down, like those of modern birds, birds aren't closely related to this branch. Ornithischians include the shovel-billed hadrosaurs, horned ceratopsians, and armored ankylosaurs. Meanwhile, animals of the Saurischia ("lizardlike hipped") branch have pubic bones that jut forward and down, including the massive long-necked sauropod *Alamosaurus*, fierce theropods like *Tyrannosaurus*, and birds.

By the time of the Aguja Formation, dinosaurs had been the primary large animals in the world for almost 100 million years, surviving multiple extinction events and changes in their species composition. The dinosaur fauna of the Aguja was made up primarily of hadrosaurs like *Aquilarhinus* ("eagle nose"); these herbivorous animals, once inaccurately known as duck-bills, were far and away the most common dinosaurs on the continent. Also present were two different families of horned dinosaurs, the big-frilled chasmosaurs like *Agujaceratops* ("horned face from the Aguja") and short-frilled centrosaurs like *Yehuecauhceratops* ("ancient horned face") from the Aguja of Mexico. Omnivorous, dome-headed pachycephalosaurs, such as *Stegoceras* ("horned roof") and armored, tanklike ankylosaurs, are also known from these environments.

Predatory dinosaurs, meanwhile, had also gone through a changing of the guard. Gone were the three-fingered allosaurs, with their claws like meat hooks. They had been replaced by tyrannosaur relatives resembling Utah's *Teratophoneus* ("monstrous murderer"), while other theropods, including the ostrichlike ornithomimids and sickle-clawed dromaeosaurs, hunted and foraged in their wake.

Mammals

The first mammals appeared during the middle of the Triassic Period and for most of the Mesozoic, mammals remained relatively small and underfoot. They nonetheless were quite diverse and successful. Multituberculates, herbivores named for the multitude of small bumps on their molars, were the most successful mammals of all time in the fossil record, a total of 130 million years. They survived the Cretaceous extinction, peaked during the Paleocene, and lived till the early Oligocene eating leaves, seeds, fruit, branches, and bark. *Cimexomys* ("bug mouse"), a tiny shrewlike hunter, and *Meniscoessus* ("little crescent tooth"), the size of a large rat or a domestic cat, were the most common multituberculate fossils found in Big Bend, known from teeth, mandibles, and an arm bone.

Insectivorous mammals were the first order of mammals to carry their babies in a placenta inside the body rather than inside pouches, like marsupials and multituberculates. With highly developed senses of smell and hearing, but poor eyesight, insectivores were nocturnal and seldom got larger than a modern rat. Their sharp incisors, canines, and tiny grinding teeth helped them devour a range of invertebrates. Their delicate bones seldom fossilize, however, and so most species—including those from Big Bend—tend to be known only from teeth. Among the unique species in the Terlingua estuaries of the Aguja were *Paleomolops langstoni* ("Langston's old rogue") and *Gallolestes agujaensis* ("Gallo Formation predator of the Aguja").

Notable Species of the Aguja Formation

Lepisosteus
(lep-ee-so-Stee-us)
("scale bone")
Order Lepisosteiformes
Family Lepisostidae

A large garfish genus. A few species of the genus survive today. These fish had a long torpedo-shaped body, a long-snouted head, and a jaw full of long, sharp serrated teeth. Their glassy, sharp scales were made of dentin, a tooth enamel coating, with a layer of inorganic bone salt called ganoine. These interlocking scales were almost impenetrable.

SIZE Up to 6.5 feet (2 meters) long, weighing about 100 pounds (45 kg).

FOSSIL HISTORY The species of gar found in the Aguja is *Lepisosteus occidentalis* ("western scale bone"), a Mesozoic species originally named in 1856 by Joseph Leidy. Remnants of *Atractosteus* ("breathing bone"), a genus that contains the modern alligator gar, are also known from this formation, as are indeterminate pieces, identified only as "gar."

BIG BEND FOSSILS Scales, teeth, skull fragments, and vertebrae, collected by William Strain and the WPA in 1938–1939, and by Wann Langston Jr. in 1970.

DIET Carnivore. Fish, cephalopods, and small aquatic prey.

NATURAL HISTORY Gar still live in fresh and brackish waters throughout North and South America, as well as the Caribbean Islands. They have retained many characteristics from their ancestors, including the ability to breathe air and an ancient sharklike digestive system. They are important predators of small aquatic prey, and larger hunters have difficulty with the gar's tough skin. The same was likely true of *Lepisosteus occidentalis*.

Scapanorhynchus
(Ska-Pan-oh-Rink-us)
("spade snout")
Order Lamniformes
Family Mitsukurinidae

A small goblin shark. It is notable for the paddle shape of its long, flat rostrum, or snout, with a combination of flat grinding teeth and wavy, sharp fangs.

SIZE Adults reached up to 13 feet (3–4 meters) long, large for a goblin shark but small in comparison with competing sharks and mosasaurs.

FOSSIL HISTORY Originally named by British paleontologist

The goblin shark ancestor *Scapanorhynchus*. This spade-nosed shark extended its complete jaw and pulled it back in when it captured fish and crustaceans on the seafloor.

James William Davis. Experts have disagreed over whether *Scapanorhynchus* was a sand shark or more akin to a goblin shark, though consensus has settled on the latter option. The only species found in Big Bend so far are *S. texanus* ("Texas spade snout") and *S. raphiodon* ("spade snout and needle tooth").

BIG BEND FOSSILS Teeth and denticles (scales like sandpaper) were collected by Thomas Lehman, Wann Langston Jr., Earl Yarmer, and Robert Rainey in 1987. A coprolite of a *Scapanorhynchus* species, identified in part by its distinctive shape, had visible undigested triangular gar scales on its surface.

DIET Carnivore. Crustaceans, cephalopods, and fish.

NATURAL HISTORY *Scapanorhynchus* likely lived in the deepest bottom of the seaway, perhaps allowing it to avoid competition with larger sharks and mosasaurs. It gave birth to live young. Modern relatives of this shark feed by extending the entire jaw out to catch prey.

Brachyrhizodus
(Brak-ee-Ree-zoe-dus)
("short snout")
Order Myliobatiformes
Family Myliobatidae

A medium-sized eagle ray. This genus is related to and closely resembles the modern cownose rays. It had a diamond-shaped body, with pectoral wings that joined the head at about eye level. The tail was whiplike and the same length as its body. Its fossil teeth were elongated hexagon shapes that locked together into flat tooth batteries, able to crush shelled invertebrates.

SIZE Reached a length of 5 feet (1–1.5 meters).

FOSSIL HISTORY Named by paleontologist Alfred Romer in 1942, *B. wichitaensis* ("short nose from Wichita") is the only species of eagle ray found so far in the Aguja Formation.

BIG BEND FOSSILS Known only from isolated teeth.

DIET Carnivore. Clams, oysters, and anything with a shell.

NATURAL HISTORY Modern eagle rays generally live in the open ocean, travel in schools, and synchronize their wing flaps to expose the mollusks in the sand below. *Brachyrhizodus* might have lived this way as well. They were preyed on by the mosasaurs, sharks, and large fish of the Interior Seaway.

Ptychotrygon
(Ty-koe-Try-gon)
("sawfishlike ray")
Order Rajiformes
Family Ptychotrygonidae

A stingray that resembled a sawfish, complete with a rostrum and spines. Its flattened body had enlarged pectoral fins that were fused, and batteries of tiny triangular shell-crushing teeth.

SIZE Up to about 12 feet long (3.7 meters) and 160 pounds (73 kg).

FOSSIL HISTORY Originally named in 1894. Fossils from this genus have been found in France, Jordan, and the United States, suggesting a global distribution. *Ptychotrygon agujaensis* ("sawfishlike stingray from the Aguja") was found abundantly in the Rattlesnake Mountain sandstone layer of the Aguja. *Ptychotrygon triangularis* ("sawfishlike stingray with triangles") is named for the shape of its teeth. This sawfish ray was the second most common species at this locality. Other *Ptychotrygon* species found in Big Bend are *P. blainensis*, *P. vermiculata*, and *P. cuspidata*.

BIG BEND FOSSILS Hundreds of teeth and fragments have been found between the various species in Big Bend.

DIET Carnivore. Shelled marine animals of all kinds.

NATURAL HISTORY *Ptychotrygon* lived in the waters near the bottom of the seaway. They were preyed on by large fish, sharks, and mosasaurs.

Onchopristis
(On-ko-Prees-tis)
("giant saw")
Order Rajiformes
Family Rajidae

An enormous sawfish. It had an elongated, flattened snout with rostral spines on either side of the saw. Each spine measured around 3.5 inches (8.9 cm) long with 2–5 barbs on each spine. This rostrum extended about a fourth of the length of its body.

SIZE Up to 21 feet (5–6 meters) long and a weight of around one ton (907 kg).

FOSSIL HISTORY Originally named by the German paleontologist Ernst Stromer in 1917, the genus has been found worldwide. Once considered to be a ray, the sawfishlike *Onchopristis* is now grouped with skates. The only species found so far in this formation is *O. dunklei* ("Dunkle's giant saw").

BIG BEND FOSSILS Extraordinarily large rostral spines that in

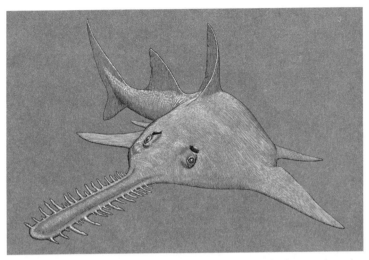

Onchopristis, a sawfish ray. This giant was as long as a telephone pole and weighed as much as a modern rhinoceros.

1986 were the largest ever seen in North America. Teeth and small sharklike dorsal fins are also known.

DIET Carnivore. Fish, mollusks, and crustaceans.

NATURAL HISTORY A bottom-dwelling ambush predator, *Onchopristis* used electroreceptors in the rostrum to detect prey. This ray may have migrated up the rivers to give birth to pups, attracting predators like mosasaurs and near-shore large fish and sharks, as well as predatory dinosaurs. Otherwise, it likely spent a great deal of time alone and submerged in sand.

Terlinguachelys
(ter-Lin-gwah-Chel-lis)
("Terlingua sea turtle")
Order Testudines
Family Protostegidae

This sea turtle was almost as large as the modern Leatherback, with longer hind limbs, a soft carapace (top shell), and reduced lower shell (plastron). The head was disproportionately large on a relatively short neck, with a sharp beak, and the tail was short.

SIZE Adults had shells about 5 feet (150 cm) long and likely weighed around 350 pounds (158 kg).

FOSSIL HISTORY *Terlinguachelys fischbecki* ("Fischbeck's turtle from Terlingua") is the only species of sea turtle found in the Big Bend area so far. The genus is named for the town of Terlingua (Spanish for "three languages"), referencing the three tongues originally spoken there, which also included Apache and English. The name was coined by paleontologists Thomas Lehman and Susan L. Tomlinson in 2004. The species name refers to George R. Fischbeck, a teacher with a weekly science show in his garage on public television in the 1960s, which both Lehman and Tomlinson enjoyed as children.

BIG BEND FOSSILS A partial skeleton included an upper and lower jaw, the hyoid (U-shaped bone that supports the tongue), carapace pieces, right half of the plastron, part of the left flipper, the right and left humerus and ulna, and the pelvic girdle. Collected in 1987 by Thomas Lehman, Wann Langston Jr. (Lehman's professor at UT-Austin), Earl Yarmer, and Robert Rainey.

DIET Omnivore. Seaweed, fish, jellyfish, squid, and crustaceans.

NATURAL HISTORY *Terlinguachelys* lived along the southern Western Interior Seaway. It may have lived a solitary life, like modern sea turtles, until it mated and traveled with others to nesting grounds. Juveniles likely hatched en masse and rushed to the sea, providing a bonanza for local carnivores. Fully grown *Terlinguachelys* were probably preyed on by mosasaurs and sharks.

Chupacabrachelys
(Chu-pa-Kob-ra-Chel-lis)
("chupacabra turtle")
Order Testudines
Family Bothremydidae

A member of an extinct family of side-necked turtles. "Side-necked" refers to the group's inability to pull the head fully into the shell. The turtle instead lines its head up sideways under the carapace.

SIZE Carapace up to 31 inches (70–80 cm) in diameter.

FOSSIL HISTORY When originally collected in 2005, *Chupacabrachelys complexus* was both a new genus and new species of side-necked turtle unique to Big Bend. The genus was named by Thomas Lehman and Steven Wick in 2010. The two were inspired by a rash of Chupacabra sightings in South Texas. One grainy photograph showed a coyote with its ears laid back, which resembled the skull of their fossil turtle. The species name refers to the Blue Man Group's Complex show, which Lehman and Wick listened to while preparing the fossils.

BIG BEND FOSSILS One of the most complete fossil specimens of this turtle species, along with a partial skeleton, skull, a nearly complete shell, a lower jaw, and isolated bones from the outer edge of the carapace called costals and peripherals.

DIET Omnivore. Fish, insects, worms, aquatic plants, amphibians, and crustaceans.

NATURAL HISTORY Side-necked turtles dominated the turtle population in the Cretaceous Period, and some remain alive today. *Chupacabrachelys* may have hunted like the modern side-necked turtle, which uses a gape-suck mechanism, slurping up aquatic prey by opening its mouth and catching anything drawn in by the sudden current. Predators were *Deinosuchus* and other crocodilians.

Aspideretes
(As-Py-der-Eets or As-Py-der-Ee-teez)
("soft-shell turtle")
Order Testudines
Family Trionychidae

A genus of small softshell turtle that persists today. It is notable for its carapace, which was smooth, leathery, and pliable on the outer edge of the shell. Softshells have a long neck with an elongated, piglike nose that acts as a snorkel, allowing the turtle to breathe while its body remains underwater. Because of the length of the neck, the turtle must be in the water to make the neck buoyant and allow food to get down the esophagus.

SIZE Carapaces range in diameter from 4 inches to about 38 inches (100 mm to less than 1 meter).

FOSSIL HISTORY Primarily known as a living genus, but carapace and plastron fossils have been found.

BIG BEND FOSSILS Many shell fragments and a rib bone. The most abundant turtle fossil in the park, found in 70–90 percent of the Big Bend fossil localities. There is not currently enough fossil evidence to determine species. Collected by Wann Langston Jr. in 1970 and Paul C. Sereno, Catherine A. Forster, and Julia T. Sankey between 1989–1991 and 2000–2007.

DIET Carnivore. Fish, insects, and amphibians.

NATURAL HISTORY As it does today, *Aspideretes* lived in the freshwater and brackish environment of a delta in places where there was soft sand or mud on the bottom. Softshell turtles still exist in Big Bend National Park near the Rio Grande. Females lay a clutch of 11–22 eggs on land between May and July. Larger members of the family are found in Africa, India, and South Asia, where they are the largest living freshwater turtles and are critically endangered.

Basilemys
(bay-Sil-eh-mis)
("king turtle")
Order Testudines
Family Nanhsiungcheylidae

A large land turtle with the limbs of a tortoise but an aquatic turtle shell. It was the largest terrestrial turtle of its time, boasting a very thick carapace with distinctive rows of pits, with three or four pits per ⅜ inch (0.9 cm). Paleontologists can identify this turtle-tortoise simply by the shell ornamentation. It had osteoderms in the skin of its legs and three claws on each of its four feet.

SIZE About 3.3 feet (1 meter) long.

FOSSIL HISTORY Named in 1876 by Edward Drinker Cope, *Basilemys* is known primarily from the western United States and Canada. Several species have subsequently been discovered, some of which preserve rare skull and neck bones, allowing for a more complete picture of the genus. Big Bend, however, has not yet produced sufficient remains to determine a species.

BIG BEND FOSSILS Partial plastron, shell fragments, and leg osteoderms were collected by Paul Sereno, Catherine Forster, and Julia Sankey in 1989–1991 and 2000–2007.

DIET Omnivore. Low-growing tough land plants, tender aquatic plants, fish, crustaceans, and insects.

NATURAL HISTORY During the Late Cretaceous, *Basilemys* crossed over the Beringia land bridge from Asia to North America, making it the only American genus known from a primarily Asian family. *Basilemys* turtles lived in the marshy area of coastal floodplain and were preyed on by freshwater alligators and other carnivorous animals and dinosaurs. The genus met its demise at the same time as the dinosaurs.

Catactegenys
(cat-Tak-eh-Gen-is)
("breaker jaw")
Order Squamata
Family Xantusiidae

A night lizard found only in the Aguja Formation of Terlingua. The head was covered in large smooth plates, and the skin was rough and granular like that of a beaded lizard. The snakelike eyes were protected by an immovable transparent membrane. Fossils show larger teeth and a greater bite force than found in modern night lizards.

SIZE Up to 5 inches (12 cm) long, slightly longer than present-day night lizards, which are 4 inches (10 cm) long.

FOSSIL HISTORY *Catactegenys solaster* ("Lone star breaking jaw") was named by Randall L. Nydam in 2013.

BIG BEND FOSSILS A lower jaw with several robust, worn teeth, collected by Randall Nydam, Timothy Rowe, and Richard Cifelli in 2013.

DIET Carnivore. Shelled animals and exoskeletons, such as bivalves, snails, crustaceans, and insects.

NATURAL HISTORY The worn jaws suggest that this animal's diet was quite rough on its teeth. Night lizards were once thought to be nocturnal—hence the name—but modern night lizards tend to live in narrow, dark rock crevices and within damp logs. Unlike most other reptiles, the night lizard gives birth to one or two live baby lizards.

Goniopholis
(Gon-ee-oh-Foe-lis)
("angled scales or scutes")
Order Crocodilia
Family Goniopholididae

A medium-sized crocodilian with a semiaquatic lifestyle similar to the American alligator. Two distinct rows of interlocking rectangular osteoderms extended from the neck to the tail, with smaller and less rectangular osteoderms on its underside. The skull revealed forward-facing eyes with keen depth perception for the pursuit of prey. Its alligator snout was rounded and wide, with short, blunt teeth used for crushing turtle shells and bones. Its front legs were much longer than its hind limbs.

SIZE Up to 13 feet (4 meters) long, weighing up to 1,653 pounds (225–750 kg).

FOSSIL HISTORY Originally named by Sir Richard Owen in 1841. *Goniopholis* remains are known from Europe and North America. The species *G. kirklandicus* was found in the Big Bend area, along with other alligator-like *Goniopholis* remains that could not be identified to the species level.

BIG BEND FOSSILS In 2019 the most complete fossil skeleton to date was found in the lower shale member, the earliest layer, of the Aguja Formation. Although it was in separate pieces, the skeleton is believed to be from one individual. Rectangular dorsal and ventral osteoderms were also found. This fossil skeleton may be named as a new genus and species in the future. It was a direct ancestor of present-day crocodilians. The remains were found by the team of Thomas Lehman, Steven Wick, Alyson B. Brink, and Thomas A. Shiller II in 2019.

DIET Carnivore. Turtles, fish, small dinosaurs, mammals, lizards, and amphibians.

NATURAL HISTORY *Goniopholis* was a solitary animal that likely lived much like modern alligators. A generalist predator, it lived in the shadow of predatory dinosaurs and larger crocodilians, such as *Deinosuchus*.

Deinosuchus
(Dy-no-Soo-kus)
("terrible crocodile")
Order Crocodilia
Family Alligatoroidea

An enormous alligatoroid. *Deinosuchus* had a long, broad, U-shaped snout equipped with robust teeth. An inflated area around the nostrils contained a second bony palate, which allowed this alligator to breathe while submerged. Four substantial limbs and the ball-and-socket joints of the vertebrae gave it the advantage of better motion and flexibility. Its body was protected

A fossil skull of the alligator ancestor *Deinosuchus (top)* beside the much smaller skull of a modern alligator.

with the heavy armor of hemispherical osteoderms ("bone skin"), plates of bone covered with skin.

SIZE Up to 39 feet (12 meters) long, about the size of an American public school bus, weighing up to 18,800 pounds (8,500 kg).

FOSSIL HISTORY The first fossils of this species were collected in 1907 by Johan A. Udden, but the subsequent 1954 find of an enormous partial jaw by the famed Barnum Brown attracted much more attention. Brown's colleagues Edwin H. Colbert and Roland "R.T." Bird originally named the animal *Phobosuchus* ("terror crocodile"), but in 1979 paleontologists Donald Baird and John R. "Jack" Horner found that it was identical to another genus, *Deinosuchus*, which had been named in 1909. In 1996, the discovery of a nearly complete skull by Thomas Lehman and James Browning allowed researchers to reconstruct the enormous alligator's head. This skull helped Wann Langston Jr. to reconstruct and cast a *Deinosuchus* at 36 feet long and 12,000 pounds. In

2020, Adam P. Cossette and Christopher A. Brochu determined that *Deinosuchus* has the characteristics of an alligatoroid.

Deinosuchus remains have been found on both sides of the Western Interior Seaway. *Deinosuchus riograndensis* ("terrible alligator near the Rio Grande") was the largest species and is the holotype, or standard, by which other species are judged. It lived primarily on the western coast of the Interior Seaway, including in Big Bend.

BIG BEND FOSSILS Many skeletons with every bone found, along with the more common teeth and osteoderms.

DIET Carnivore. *Deinosuchus* seems to have had a particular taste for turtles; tooth marks from its jaws have been found on fossilized shells of side-necked turtles like *Chupacabrachelys* and sea turtles like *Terlinguachelys*. Bite marks have been found on a hadrosaur's tail vertebrae fossilized in the Aguja Formation of Coahuila, Mexico, suggesting that adults also ate dinosaurs.

NATURAL HISTORY *Deinosuchus* was the apex predator of this time and the largest carnivore known from the Aguja ecosystem. Like modern alligators, it was a semiaquatic ambush predator that grabbed its prey from the banks, dragged the animal into the water, and likely drowned it with a death roll. Like modern saltwater crocodiles, *Deinosuchus* seems to have been comfortable in saltwater and estuarine environments and might have traveled surprising distances in the open ocean. Although nothing is known of its parental care, modern alligators take excellent care of their eggs and young; *Deinosuchus* likely did, too. Young individuals were prey to carnivorous dinosaurs, mosasaurs, and sharks.

Aquilarhinus
(ah-Quill-ah-Rye-nus)
("eagle nose")
Order Ornithischia
Family Hadrosauridae

A flat-headed, big-nosed hadrosaurine dinosaur. It had a distinctive "roman nose" shape to its nasal crest, and it could use its W-shaped jaw to shovel out vegetation. Its forelimbs ended in mittenlike paws, and its hind limbs in broad three-toed feet.

Hadrosaurs ("bulky lizards") were a large, diverse family of browsing dinosaurs with long, shovel-billed jaws and—in some families—large cranial crests. They were able to move on either two legs or four, depending on the height needed to get to plant material. Despite a reputation in most dinosaur art as passive victims, many grew to formidable sizes and were not animals to be trifled with.

SIZE Up to 30 feet (9 meters) long, 9 feet (2.7 meters) tall, weighing 6,600 pounds (3,000 kg).

Aquilarhinus palimentus feeding in shallow water. This noncrested hadrosaur used its W-shaped bottom jaw like a shovel to scoop up watery vegetation in its coastal environment.

FOSSIL HISTORY *Aquilarhinus palimentus* ("eagle nose with a shovel chin") was discovered in 2019 by Thomas Lehman from the WPA quarry findings of 1938–1939. It is currently the only species found.

BIG BEND FOSSILS Skull and neck fragments, nasal crests, upturned "shovel" jawbone, a pelvis bone, a nearly complete left hand or front paw, and parts of one back paw with toes and claws. Collected by discoverer Thomas Lehman, Neil La Fon, and Kyle L. Davies in 1983, with additional material by Jonathan R. Wagner in 1999.

DIET Herbivore. A wide variety of plants at different heights on land and in water.

NATURAL HISTORY *Aquilarhinus* lived on the coastlines, foraging in swamps and around shallow streams. These hadrosaurs likely traveled in herds for protection. The arched nose may have housed inflatable air sacs for display and resonating honks. Its distinctive bill suggests that it lived and foraged in a manner unlike other known hadrosaurines, but more fossils are needed to clarify its ecology.

Angulomastacator daviesi
(an-Goo-low-Mass-tuh-Kay-tor)
("Davies's bend chewer")
Order Ornithischia
Family Hadrosauridae

A new genus and species of a one-of-a-kind crested hadrosaur.

SIZE In the absence of adequate fossils, the size and head crest cannot be determined.

FOSSIL HISTORY A partial left maxilla with teeth positioned in a 45-degree angle was discovered in the early 1980s by Kyle Davies, a Big Bend hadrosaur expert. The genus was named by Jonathan Wagner and Thomas Lehman in 2009. "Angulo" refers to the bend of the Rio Grande where this unique fossil was found,

The crested hadrosaur *Angulomastacator*. No other hadrosaur found in Big Bend had a jaw that bent like this.

as well as to the angle of the jaw. The species name refers to Dr. Davies, who was the first to suggest that a crested lambeosaurine hadrosaur could be present in the Aguja Formation.

DIET Herbivore. Aquatic and terrestrial plants that could be reached with two- and four-leg stances.

NATURAL HISTORY Lived near the coastal water's edge and nested on a high ridge to watch for predators. These hadrosaurs were like huge present-day chickens, and they were on the menu for many dinosaurs.

Aguja Ankylosaur (Euoplocephalus)
(Yoo-ah-Plo-sef-ah-lus)
("well-armed head")
Order Ornithischia
Family Ankylosauridae

A large ankylosaur known only from scrappy remains. It is possibly referable to the genus *Euoplocephalus*. The family is notable for its bone-clubbed tail, barrel-shaped body, four powerful legs, and wide inverted triangular skull with two large horns on either side.

SIZE Up to 23 feet (7 meters) long, 8 feet (2.4 meters) wide, weighing about 5,000 pounds (2,268 kg).

FOSSIL HISTORY The genus was originally named by Lawrence Lambe in 1910 from Canadian fossils, with only a single species, *E. tutus* ("well-armed head safely protected"), a famous ankylosaur. Fossil remains of other ankylosaurs in North America have often been assigned to this genus, a practice that has been the subject of some disagreement. The genus may be more properly split into multiple taxa.

BIG BEND FOSSILS Osteoderms, vertebrae, phalanges (finger or toe bones), and a metapodial (long bone in the hand or foot that connects to the digits) were collected by the WPA and William Strain in 1938–1939 and Barnum Brown and R. T. Bird in 1940. The remains were assigned to *Euoplocephalus tutus* but may represent a different species or genus.

DIET Herbivore. Low-growing ferns, cycads, and flowering plants; relatively tough, fibrous material that other dinosaurs could not process.

NATURAL HISTORY *Euoplocephalus* and related ankylosaurs likely spent most of their time in solitary wanderings or among small groups. Its complicated nasal passages may have allowed for an enhanced sense of smell or a mammal-like ability to warm air before fully breathing it. Although it was bulky, researchers have suggested that *Euoplocephalus* and its relatives might have been able to move as quickly as a modern rhino or hippopotamus. The large tail club likely played a role in defense and intraspecies dustups.

Panoplosaurus
(Pan-oh-Ploe-saw-rus)
("completely armored lizard")
Order Ornithischia
Family Nodosauridae

A large, heavily armored nodosaur. Horizontal osteoderm bands studded with nodules and spines covered the shoulders and back. Oval osteoderms covered the short neck, shoulders, and front limbs. The helmetlike head even had thick, bony cheek plates. The snout was short and narrow, helping it root through the plants on the ground. Leaf-shaped teeth were numerous and rigid and could slice through low-growing vegetation.

Nodosaurs belong to the same group as the ankylosaurs, but their pattern of armor is different, and they lack a tail club. Notable nodosaurs from Cretaceous North America include *Panoplosaurus* and *Edmontonia*. Both genera have fossil material currently assigned to them in Big Bend.

SIZE Up to 23 feet (7 meters) long, 6.6 feet (2 meters) tall, weighing in at 3,500 pounds (1,587 kg).

FOSSIL HISTORY Also named by Lawrence Lambe in 1919, *Panoplosaurus mirus* ("wonderous completely armored lizard") is one of several groups of armored dinosaurs originally discovered in the Dinosaur Park Formation of Alberta; other fossils were discovered later in the United States. *Edmontonia* ("one from Edmonton Formation") and *Panoplosaurus* are the only nodosaurs found in Big Bend so far.

BIG BEND FOSSILS Scapula and osteoderms were collected by Barnum Brown and Roland T. Bird in 1940 and J. Willis Stovall and Wann Langston Jr. in 1950.

DIET Herbivore. Low-level grasses, shrubs, bushes, and small flowering trees.

NATURAL HISTORY *Panoplosaurus* likely lived a somewhat

An armored *Panoplosaurus*. The armor was made of bone sheathed in keratin.

solitary life, the same as other armored dinosaurs. Even without tail clubs, fully grown adults had armor that would have presented a formidable challenge to predators, such as the resident tyrannosaurs and *Deinosuchus*. Like most herbivores and present-day hoofed animals, this dinosaur digested its plant material with fermentation. *Panoplosaurus* was also one of the last nodosaurs known to exist before the extinction event 66 mya.

Agujaceratops
(ah-Goo-Ha-Ser-rah-tops)
("Aguja horn face")
Order Ornithischia
Family Ceratopsidae

A ceratopsian dinosaur with a horned head, parrotlike beak, and heavy frill. *Agujaceratops* belonged to a subfamily of ceratopsians called the chasmosaurines, notable for their particularly showy frills. The frill of *Agujaceratops* made up a third of its body length, and a fossilized skull from this animal discovered in Big Bend is the largest ceratopsid skull ever discovered.

The frill had six very large scalloped bones on the top edge and was circled with blunt hornlets. Two long, solid horns perched on the dinosaur's brow, which lengthened as the animal grew and likely differed in position depending on the sex. A single short rostral horn sat in front of the long, narrow beak. The beak snipped off low-growing vegetation as its slicing teeth moved scissorlike through bulky vegetation. The body was large and compact, with longer hind limbs and five-toed forelimbs.

SIZE Up to 21 feet (7 meters) long, weighing about 6,000 pounds (2,700 kg).

FOSSIL HISTORY Originally identified as an unnamed ceratopsian in the WPA quarries of 1938–1939, the animal was named *Chasmosaurus mariscalensis* ("opening lizard") by paleontologist Thomas Lehman. The skull's frill had large openings on either side and resembled the *Chasmosaurus* fossils found in Canada by Lawrence Lambe. The species name *mariscalensis* ("from the Mariscal Mountain") referred to the area where the fossil was found.

Paleontologists Spencer G. Lucas, Robert M. Sullivan, and Adrian Hunt reanalyzed the animal in 2006, to be split into a new genus and designated Agujaceratops mariscalensis as the type species to which all specimens are compared.

In 2016, Thomas Lehman, Steven Wick, and Kenneth Barnes identified and named a new species, *Agujaceratops mavericus* ("Maverick Aguja horned face"). One of a kind, a maverick, it was named also for the park's Old Maverick Road. Thus far two species of *Agujaceratops* are known in Big Bend. *Agujaceratops* was the most common type of ceratopsid found in the park and is the oldest known chasmosaurine ceratopsian in North America so far.

BIG BEND FOSSILS Known from a nearly complete skeleton

Agujaceratops, an inhabitant of the Big Bend area when it looked more like Galveston Island. The head of one from Big Bend, with its massive frill, is the largest of its family found so far in North America.

along with a braincase, a horn-core from above the left eye, left maxilla (upper jaw) and right dentary (lower jaw), right cora-coid (part of the scapula), and a pelvic bone. Collected by Wann Langston Jr. in 1938—the most complete skeleton yet recovered—and the WPA and William Strain in 1938–1939. Further remains were recovered by Paul Sereno, Catherine Forster, and Julia

Sankey in 1989–1991 and 2000–2007, and Kenneth Barnes throughout the 2000s.

DIET Herbivore. Low-growing plants like cycads, ferns, flowering shrubs; possibly supplementing its diet on carrion.

NATURAL HISTORY *Agujaceratops* lived in the swampy coastal floodplains and forests. During the WPA excavation, researchers collected a rare bone bed of 20 young and adult chasmosaurine ceratopsids, suggesting that they traveled in herds and that their appearance differed according to age and sex. Little ceratopsids likely traveled with the herd until they were grown. *Agujaceratops* may have been preyed on by tyrannosaurs or *Deinosuchus*, but fully grown adults would have been formidable customers, and predators would have been wise to keep away.

Texacephale
(Tex-ah-Sef-ah-lee)
("Texas head")
Order Ornithischia
Family Pachycephalosauridae

A small pachycephalosaur, a dinosaur with a bone-domed skull up to 10 inches (25.4 cm) thick. Its beaked jaws contained peg-like front teeth to crop plants, and there were small, triangular teeth with jagged edges on the front and back of the crowns. *Texacephale* walked on two legs and had shortened arms, with four digits on each limb. The neck was short and thick, and its body had a bulky torso suitable for digesting plant material, reminiscent of present-day ruminators like deer and goats.

SIZE About the size of a medium dog.

FOSSIL HISTORY *Texacephale langstoni* ("Langston's Texas head") was discovered by Darren Tanke in 2008 at the WPA-Quarry 1, where the bone bed of 20 individual *Agujaceratops* was found. This rare skullcap fossil was tossed away previously because it resembled a rock. The species was named by paleontologists Nicholas R. Longrich, Julia Sankey, and Darren Tanke in honor of Wann Langston Jr. for his contributions to vertebrate paleontology and the fossil record in Big Bend National Park.

BIG BEND FOSSILS A complete skeleton is unknown; the animal is currently known only from teeth and skull fragments. Partial skull and teeth were collected by the WPA and William Strain, 1938–1939, and by Darren Tanke in 2008.

DIET Omnivore. Mostly plant material (seeds, nuts, stems, leaves, and fruit), but likely also took small animals such as lizards and mammals, as well as possibly scavenging on carrion.

NATURAL HISTORY A small generalist browser, *Texacephale langstoni* lived in the dense vegetation of the coastal marsh and near the shore of the Western Interior Seaway. It seems to have

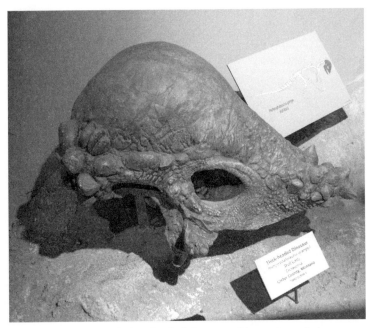

A fossil skull the size of a bowling ball, from an older pachycephalosaur.

been endemic to southwestern North America and distinct from other pachycephalosaurs in the northern regions of the continent. The usage of the domed skull in pachycephalosaurs is up for debate, though it is now clear that their skulls changed considerably as they aged, with younger animals having flatter skulls. The domes may have been used for sexual signaling or ramming behaviors, as seen in modern goats. *Texacephale* was likely preyed on by dromaeosaurs, tyrannosauroids of all sizes, and large alligators like *Deinosuchus*.

Stegoceras
(Steg-goh-Ser-as)
("horn roof")
Order Ornithischia
Family Pachycephalosauridae

A bipedal dome-headed pachycephalosaur, small to medium-sized compared with other dinosaurs of its kind. Its dome was thick but flatter than the dome of *Texacephale*, surrounded with ornamental round outgrowths that formed a fringe on the sides and back. The dome increased in roundness as the animal matured, but the ornaments eroded with age.

Stegoceras held its triangular head, neck, back, and tail stiff and parallel to the ground. Its arms were short, like those of *Tyrannosaurus rex*, but it had four digits on each hand and foot.

SIZE Up to about 8 feet (2.5 meters) long, weighing almost 90 pounds (40 kg).

FOSSIL HISTORY The first *Stegoceras* domes were collected and named by Lawrence Lambe in 1902. *Stegoceras validum* ("strong horn roof") remained the only identified species until 2011, when *S. novomexicanum* was found in New Mexico.

BIG BEND FOSSILS Relatively pristine teeth were recovered in the park. The teeth were small, serrated, and recurved. They did

Stegoceras was smaller than *Texacephale* and still had sharp, serrated teeth millions of years later.

not form a straight cutting row, overlapping toward the back of the mouth.

DIET Omnivore. Mostly plant material, but possibly an opportunistic predator or scavenger as well.

NATURAL HISTORY This pachycephalosaur was small compared with other dinosaurs in the area, so it was at a constant disadvantage in the predator-prey rivalry.

Stegoceras is not to be confused with *Stegosaurus* ("roof lizard") from the Stegosauridae family. No *Stegosaurus* dinosaur fossils have been found in Big Bend so far.

Aguja Ornithomimids
(or-Nith-oh-Mime-ids)
("bird mimics")
Order Saurischia
Family Ornithomimidae

A group of theropod dinosaurs that closely resemble but are not related to modern ostriches. They were feathered and had a slender toothless beak in a small skull, large eyes, long and powerful hind legs, and a body-length stiff tail for counterbalance. Ornithomimid fossil material known from Big Bend is assigned to one of two genera, *Struthiomimus* ("ostrich mimic") and *Ornithomimus* ("bird mimic").

Struthiomimus had a long neck that made up 40 percent of its ostrich-shaped body. On its long, slender arms, the forearm was immobile. The three fingers on each hand were mildly opposable; one finger had limited movement while the other two fingers worked as a single unit. It may have used the slightly curved claws to hook and bring down branches, as a sloth does. The feet were tipped with three short toes bearing hooflike claws.

Ornithomimus had a smaller body with a shorter torso, long slender arms, and robust forearms. Its three slothlike claws and fingers were all the same length and were able to move independently of each other. Its top jaw was able to open upward against the skull, which allowed the dinosaur to consume larger food.

SIZE *Struthiomimus:* up to 19 feet (5.8 meters) long and 6.4 feet (1.9 meters) high at the hips, weighing 930 pounds (150–420 kg). *Ornithomimus:* up to 13.2 feet (4 meters) long, 7 feet (2.1 meters) high, weighing about 370 pounds (161 kg).

FOSSIL HISTORY *Struthiomimus* was named in 1902 by Lawrence Lambe, and *Ornithomimus* was named by famed American paleontologist Othniel Charles Marsh. Both researchers noted the hollow bones and other birdlike features of the animals, which inspired the names. Somewhat later, as researchers found more evidence that birds evolved from dinosaurs, some speculated that ornithomimids might have been feathered, which was confirmed by the discovery of multiple specimens of *Ornithomimus* with feather traces in 1995, 2008, and 2009.

BIG BEND FOSSILS *Struthiomimus* is known from the skull and parts of the upper and lower leg bones, though these have not been assigned to a specific species. *Ornithomimus* is known from femur and pelvis fragments, bones of the feet, tail vertebrae, and other postcranial bones.

The remains were collected by William Strain and the WPA, in 1938–1939, and by Paul Sereno, Catherine Forster, and Julia Sankey in 1989–1991 and 2000–2007.

DIET Omnivores. As theropods, they fed on small vertebrates, eggs, and plant material, or they scavenged. They digested their food through gut fermentation as herbivores do today.

NATURAL HISTORY The sociability of these animals is still largely unknown, but some ornithomimids have been preserved in what may be family groups. As adaptable generalist browsers, they were a likely prey item for crocodiles and larger theropods,

Ornithomimus. This creature was very similar to an emu both in appearance and in its ability to run rapidly away from predators.

but their speed would have made them difficult to catch. *Struthiomimus* was one of the fastest dinosaurs of the Cretaceous Period, potentially able to reach speeds between 31 and 50 mph (50–80 km/h) when threatened; *Ornithomimus* was also fast, with speeds of up to 30 mph (48 km/h).

Leptorhynchos
(Lep-toh-Rink-kose)
("slim snout")
Order Saurischia
Family Caenagnathidae

A flightless feathered dinosaur with a distinctive beak and crest. This genus belongs to a group related to the more famous Mongolian *Oviraptor*. It had a short, boxy skull with a slightly upturned beak, slender arms with skinny claws, and long, graceful legs.

SIZE Roughly the size of a turkey.

FOSSIL HISTORY *Leptorhynchos gaddisi* ("Gaddis's slim snout") was named by Nicholas Longrich in 2013, after the Gaddis family, on whose land the fossil was found.

BIG BEND FOSSIL A small, short, and deep mandible with a rounded chin, dated to 75 mya.

DIET Omnivore. Vegetation, fruit, and small animals like lizards and mammals.

NATURAL HISTORY Caenagnathids like *Leptorhynchos* had longer, shallower jaws than their oviraptor cousins, and their build was considerably lighter, suggesting a lifestyle adapted for speed rather than rough-and-tumble defense. The head crest and feathers might have been brightly colored for social signaling. Their cousins the oviraptors were excellent parents and brooded their eggs, and *Leptorhynchos* may have done so as well. It was probably preyed on by crocodiles, dromaeosaurs, and young tyrannosaurs swift enough to catch it.

Saurornitholestes
(Saw-roh-or-Nith-oh-Less-teez)
("lizard bird thief")
Order Saurischia
Family Dromaeosauridae

A medium-sized predatory feathered dinosaur. It had a slight build and long legs with a stiff, slender, and lengthy tail. Its skull was long and low with large forward-facing eyes, and the snout was upturned. The dinosaur had a powerful sense of smell. Its jaws contained widely spaced, recurved fangs and flat preening teeth in the front. The large hands had three long fingers that ended in strongly curved claws. Dromaeosaurs like *Saurornitholestes* are famous for their feet: The second toe had a large sickle-shaped claw held aloft from the ground. The third and fourth toes supported the weight of the dinosaur as it walked or ran. *Saurornitholestes* was feathered and warm-blooded like present-day birds.

SIZE Up to 6 feet (1.8 meters) long, 2 feet (0.6 meters) high, weighing about 22 pounds (10 kg).

FOSSIL HISTORY *Saurornitholestes langstoni* ("Langston's lizard bird thief") was named by Hans-Dieter Sues in 1978, in honor of Wann Langston Jr., a beloved paleontologist and professor at UT-Austin. The species is occasionally equated with the Mongolian *Velociraptor*, an animal it closely resembled, but a 2014 study of a nearly complete specimen by Philip J. Currie and Clive Coy of the Royal Ontario Museum in Canada showed that *Saurornitholestes* had a shorter and deeper skull than its Asian counterpart.

BIG BEND FOSSILS Many teeth, femur, tibia, fibula, eggshells, and bones of hatchlings, juveniles, and adults were collected by William Strain and the WPA project in 1938–1939, and by Paul Sereno, Catherine Forster, and Julia Sankey in 1989–1991 and 2000–2007. According to Dr. Sankey, the fossil teeth were still sharp millions of years later and were the most abundant fossil found in the locality she studied in Big Bend National Park.

A dromaeosaur (*Saurornitholestes*) pursuing a small mammal (*Alphadon*). The bird relative *Saurornitholestes* was a cousin of the Mongolian *Velociraptor*. The genus *Alphadon* includes a diverse group of marsupials that lived and hunted day and night in the coastal Big Bend.

DIET Carnivore. Smaller dinosaurs, reptiles, amphibians, and mammals, as well as scavenged carrion when available.

NATURAL HISTORY A widespread, opportunistic, and successful animal, *Saurornitholestes* seemingly preferred wetter environments around estuaries, rivers, and lakes. Although the sickle claw has been hypothesized in the past to be a tearing weapon, modern studies suggest it was used in the same manner as modern raptors, such as owls, do, to climb, grip, and puncture prey. New evidence shows that they were also capable of using the long claws to dig underground for prey.

Aguja Tyrannosaurine
(Ty-RAN-no-Saw-reen)
("of the tyrant lizard family")
Order Saurischia
Family Tyrannosauridae

A large predatory dinosaur with a big head and small arms specialized for tackling big game. Smaller and thinner than the more familiar *Tyrannosaurus rex*, it may have resembled animals like *Albertosaurus* and Utah's *Teratophoneus*. The record of specimens from Big Bend is currently too poor to assign a genus.

SIZE About 21 feet (6.5 meters) long, weighing about 1,543 pounds (700 kg).

The Aguja Tyrannosaurine. Fossils of this dinosaur and its relatives are rare, suggesting that tyrannosaur numbers were kept low by the colossal alligator *Deinosuchus* and its relatives.

FOSSIL HISTORY Remains of the Aguja Tyrannosaurine were collected by Paul Sereno, Catherine Forster, and Julia Sankey in 1989–1991 and 2000–2007, and by Thomas Lehman and Steven Wick in 2012.

BIG BEND FOSSILS Most commonly known from complete and fragmented teeth, but also from frontals (the bones of the forehead) and a sagittal crest (a ridge of bone in the middle of the skull that runs from front to back, signaling extremely strong jaw muscles). Tail vertebrae, a lower leg bone, and foot bones have also been found.

DIET Carnivore. Hadrosaurs, young ceratopsians, and smaller dinosaurs.

NATURAL HISTORY Like modern warm-blooded predators with healthy appetites, the Aguja Tyrannosaurine likely patrolled large territories. Tyrannosauroids seemed to change remarkably as they grew, with youngsters significantly more fleet-footed and swift than the bulkier adults. It seems likely that they targeted different prey as they aged, with younger animals pursuing ornithomimids and larger relatives tackling hadrosaurs, thereby squeezing out medium-sized dinosaurian predators. Although tyrannosaurs are generally considered apex predators of any ecosystem they inhabited, the 40-foot crocodilians present in the time of the Aguja Formation seem to have offered stiff competition; their numbers are rare.

Alphadon
(Al-fah-don)
("first tooth")
Class Metatheria
Family Alphadontidae

A small marsupial mammal. It likely had a strong sense of smell and hearing but poor eyesight. Many species of *Alphadon* have been found throughout the Aguja, the Javelina, and the Cretaceous Black Peaks Formations. (See illustration under *Saurornitholestes* earlier in this chapter.)

SIZE About 12 inches (30 cm) long, weighing about 12 ounces (340 g).

FOSSIL HISTORY The first *Alphadon* fossils were originally found in China by George Gaylord Simpson in 1929, and multiple species have subsequently been named. They are known only from scrappy remains—mostly teeth—due to the delicate nature of the tiny bones. *Alphadon perexiguus* ("very small first tooth") is a typical Big Bend example and is thus far known only from the Terlingua area. Other Big Bend species are *A. marshi*, *A. halleyi*, and *A. sahnii*.

BIG BEND FOSSILS Teeth collected by Barbara R. Standhardt in 1986; Paul Sereno, Catherine Forster, and Julia Sankey in 1989–1991 and 2000–2007; Richard Cifelli in 1994; and Julia Sankey in 1998.

DIET Omnivore. Insects, fruit, seeds, bird eggs, smaller rodents and lizards, invertebrates, and scavenged already dead animals.

NATURAL HISTORY *Alphadon* occupied an enormous range of ecological niches on land, in burrows, and in trees, where they could be protected from carnivores of all sizes. This mammal was related to modern marsupials but vanished in the extinction of the dinosaurs.

JAVELINA AND CRETACEOUS BLACK PEAKS FORMATIONS
Latest Cretaceous
from 72 Ma (Late Campanian Age) to 66 Ma (Maastrichtian Age)
Time Traveler's Field Notes: 67 mya, August 19, 4:00 pm
150 miles inland from the Western Interior Seaway

IT'S BRUTALLY HOT. YOU ARE STANDING IN THE SHADE OF A SMALL copse of trees on a broad seasonal floodplain, a landscape cut through with small washes and shallow arroyos. Other clusters of evergreen trees stand in ragged lines along sun-bleached meadows of fern and bracken; heat dances over the fern prairies beneath a cloudless blue sky. In the distance, a group of *Alamosaurus* giants—one of the last and largest of the long-necked sauropod dinosaurs in North America—wander among the copses, their brightly colored necks like 32-foot billboards as they browse the upper canopies. Scattered hadrosaurs graze nearby, their honks and rumbles drifting over the still air. In your bones, you can feel a slight buzz; the song of the *Alamosaurus* is too low for the human ear, an ultrasound rumble that can carry for miles.

Alamosaurus is one of the primary engineers of this ecosystem, large enough to bulldoze trees and keep the fern prairies open against encroaching forests. Those that survive to adulthood can reach truly titanic sizes. But even giants die eventually. Ahead of you, a 90-ton mountain of flesh rises up from the ground. An old *Alamosaurus* has succumbed to some internal ailment, leaving behind a carcass nearly 100 feet long. The body has been sitting out in the heat for several days, and in the still air, the smell is truly pervasive, a heavy odor of sour rot and spoiled meat that sits heavy in the throat. Some of the odor is from the gases of decomposition, which—as in modern whale-falls—can build up enough under the right circumstances to explode, volleying gobbets of rotten meat and viscera high into the air and hundreds of feet over the surroundings.

Disgusting as it is, staking out a dead *Alamosaurus* provides a perfect opportunity to see a broad cross-section of local wildlife. Several hundred feet away from the body, a 29-foot tyrannosaur dozes in the dappled shade of a stand of trees, his belly round and taut as a drum. The tyrannosaur could never have brought down an adult *Alamosaurus*, and finding this relatively fresh carcass has been an absolute bonanza. He's been hanging around for days, waking only to gorge himself.

Other scavengers are working the carcass over as well. A band of mottled *Bravoceratops*—big-horned, big-frilled ceratopsians— are tearing strips of flesh off an enormous leg bone with their sharp beaks, taking advantage of the windfall to add a bit of protein to their otherwise herbivorous diet. The enormous body is swarming with flies, insects, and beetles, and this, in turn, attracts lizards and small mammals, which attract small sickle-clawed dromaeosaurs like *Saurornitholestes*. One mother has shown up leading a squadron of peeping, puffball chicks. As she feeds, she keeps one eye on them as they chase insects in the shadow of the massive tail.

A different type of shadow passes over the plain, and the *Saurornitholestes* crouches down, pressing herself against the decaying flesh. Her chicks freeze. A moment later, a giraffe-sized pterosaur touches down in a puff of dust, stilt-walking over on folded wings. This is *Quetzalcoatlus*, one of the largest pterosaurs ever to exist. Its long bill is a furious red, and its body is covered in brilliant white fuzz. It moves with a curious, jerky movement on the ground, like a hunting stork. It cocks its head, considering the gaping chest cavity with a gimlet eye; then its neck strikes down, bill spearing into the moist darkness inside the body.

It will be a week before scavengers abandon the carcass, the choice scraps picked off the heavy bones, the merciless sun baking the remaining flesh into rawhide too tough to appeal. For now, however, the fallen *Alamosaurus* is a buffet in a world of giants, an intersection of some of the largest land animals currently on

Earth. They are supremely well adapted to thrive in an incredibly complex ecosystem.

And all of them are doomed.

GEOLOGY OF THE JAVELINA AND CRETACEOUS BLACK PEAKS FORMATIONS

The Javelina Formation resulted from the deposition of river sands of ancient stream channels, interbedded with muds representing floods overtopping the channel banks. Mudstones and ancient soils created in these floods took on colors according to the chemicals in the rocks that were eroded into soils of the time.

The different colors of soil help researchers determine more about various phases of Javelina's ecosystem. Purple colors mark the presence of phosphorus and potassium, representing fertile soil during a warm climate with abundant rainfall. Gray and olive-green colors represent water saturation and lack of oxygen in the soil (anoxia), due to a loss of iron minerals from seawater covering the soil. Red represents periods of slow dehydration and highly oxygenated soil, along with hematite that gives the soil its red color. These different-colored layers are visible as you drive through the park and surrounding areas.

The environment of the Javelina was warm but not strongly seasonal, with suggestions of long periods (perhaps thousands of years) of aridity, alternated with extended periods with more humid conditions.

The Cretaceous interval of the Black Peaks Formation, meanwhile, represents the deposits of an inland floodplain. Its key features are flooding, the deposition of river sediments, and erosion. There are layers of dark bands of red and black mudstones that are interrupted by river sands. Vertebrate fossils are uncommon except for fish, reptiles, and the occasional huge dinosaur. The Cretaceous Black Peaks is located in the lower one-third of the Black Peaks Formation.

WHERE TO SEE THE JAVELINA AND CRETACEOUS BLACK PEAKS FORMATIONS

You can see the Javelina along the northwest portion of Chimneys Trail, and west of the Highway 118 park entrance sign, near Maverick entrance station. Another Javelina outcrop can be seen to the west of the spot where Glenn Springs Road meets River Road at mile 8.5 and Big Gap turnoff at mile 8.6.

The Black Peaks Formation, meanwhile, is visible along Tornillo Flat and from the Fossil Discovery Exhibit.

FOSSIL REMAINS OF THE JAVELINA AND CRETACEOUS BLACK PEAKS FORMATIONS

Plants

More than 300 different fossil plants are found in the Javelina Formation. Logs and log fragments of 2 feet (60 cm) in diameter along an ancient river's edge represent the remains of a flowering tree called *Javelinoxylon multisporum* ("tree with lots of spores from the Javelina Formation") that was at least 90 feet (27 meters) tall. Termite excrement—called frass—was found in galleries created inside *Javelinoxylon*'s trunk. The fossilized trees don't have defined tree rings, which suggests that the trees grew in an environment without seasonal changes in water availability; however, the large number of storage cells in trees from the Cretaceous Big Bend suggests that these trees may have stored water like succulents.

A new species of bald cypress was found by Steven Wick; it was named *Sabinoxylon wicki* ("Wick's Sabino cypress tree") in his honor. *Tornilloxylon maxwellii* ("Maxwell's screw bean tree") was an evergreen much like the mesquite. Fossilized fern, maple, and palm leaves have also been found in the Javelina, along with seeds, spores, and pollen.

Reptiles

Several families of lizards continued to persist from the Aguja

Formation, including whiptails, monitor lizards, and night lizards. Snakes known from the area include *Dunnophis microechinis* ("tiny spine"), an extinct genus of dwarf boa. A small nonvenomous constricting snake, *Dunnophis* was nocturnal and spent the day burrowed underground. It survived into the Eocene Epoch, and the family persists today in the West Indies, Mexico, and south to Brazil.

Also present was *Champsosaurus*, a reptile that resembled crocodiles but belonged to a distant lineage of reptiles with no living relatives.

Pterosaurs

The oldest of the flying vertebrates, pterosaurs evolved at around the same time as their sister group, the dinosaurs. Initial fossils discovered from the fine-grained deposits of Bavaria confused naturalists, who wondered if the small animals used their strange wings to swim. By the 1800s, however, paleontologists understood that pterosaurs flew, although there was much debate about how efficient they were in the air. The mechanics of pterosaur flight remain a bit of a mystery, but they were clearly successful and sophisticated animals, as diverse pterosaur families survived for nearly 150 million years before the Cretaceous extinction.

With hollow bones and wings supported by an elongated fourth finger, pterosaurs ranged in size from the tiny *Anuragnathus* ("frog face") to the famous *Pteranodon* and the immense azhdarchid pterosaurs of the Late Cretaceous. Pterosaurs undoubtedly soared through the skies of Big Bend prior to the Javelina Formation, but the most famous from the area is *Quetzalcoatlus*, a pterosaur with a 36-foot wingspan that is one of the jewels of Big Bend's fossil record.

Dinosaurs

The dinosaur fauna of the Javelina was somewhat similar to that of the Aguja Formation, with the hadrosaur *Kritosaurus*, chasmosaurine ceratopsians such as *Bravoceratops*, and the continued presence of dromaeosaurs like *Saurornitholestes*. The conversion of swampy delta forests to occasionally arid floodplains, however, opened opportunities for new animals, including giant sauropods like *Alamosaurus* and an as-yet-unnamed species of *Tyrannosaurus*. Bird species with teeth and feathers are known from both the Javelina and the Black Peaks Formations, but the evidence is too scrappy to assign a genus and species.

Mammals

Multituberculates (herbivores with bumpy teeth) and insectivores were also a part of this formation. In addition to species persisting from the Aguja, the Javelina yielded tooth fossils and a few crushed skulls from a primate ancestor called *Palaechthon nacimienti*, with widely spaced, forward-facing predator eyes and a keen sense of smell. This arboreal insectivore likely hunted insects and eggs both on the ground and in the trees and managed to survive the extinction of the dinosaurs, going extinct 63.3 mya in the Paleocene.

Notable Species of the Javelina and Cretaceous Black Peaks Formations

Dasyatis
(Das-ee-Ah-tis)
("rough skate")
Order Myliobatiformes
Family Dasyatidae

A whiptail stingray with diamond-shaped pectoral fins. The body was wider than it was long. It had small eyes and very large spiracles behind the eyes. Its single serrated venomous stinger sat on top of the base of its tail.

SIZE About 18 inches (45 cm) long.

FOSSIL HISTORY *Dasyatis matrixi* ("rough skate from fine-grained rock") was named from living members of the genus in 1810.

BIG BEND FOSSILS Vertebrae and small triangular teeth in the Aguja and Cretaceous Black Peaks Formations.

DIET Carnivore. Squid, mollusks, fish, and crustaceans.

NATURAL HISTORY *Dasyatis* lived in tropical or temperate sandy and muddy brackish waters less than 328 feet (100 meters) deep. The stingray was preyed on by sharks and large fish. It gave birth to live young through eggs incubated and hatched inside the female's body. Present-day whiptail stingrays can grow to giant proportions, and some are able to go on land and breathe air for about 5 minutes.

Habrosaurus
(Hab-roh-Saw-rus)
("splendid lizard")
Order Urodela
Family Sirenidae

A fully aquatic, eel-like salamander, the oldest and largest siren genus yet known. It had tiny forelimbs with three digits and no hind limbs or pelvis. Its upper jaw contained teeth with bulky crowns for crushing hard shells. Feathery external gills on its neck allowed it to breathe underwater. The eyes were situated in the skull, on the roof of the mouth.

SIZE Between 2 and 3 feet (61–91 cm) long.

FOSSIL HISTORY Named by Charles Gilmore in 1933, *Habrosaurus dilatus* ("splendid lizard with larger eyes") was originally considered to be a reptile before being identified as an amphibian.

BIG BEND FOSSILS A partial atlas—the first cervical (neck) bone—was collected by Barbara Standhardt in 1986.

DIET Shell-eating carnivore. Insects, crustaceans, and arachnids, as well as carrion.

NATURAL HISTORY *Habrosaurus dilatus* existed in slow-moving rivers, lakes, and ponds, where it laid eggs in the water like other amphibians. Able to breathe through its skin, it likely was primarily active at night, as are modern sirens, and could come on land during unusually wet conditions. It was preyed on by fish, alligators, and turtles, and survived for a short while after the extinction of dinosaurs.

Suffosio
(suf-Fose-Ee-oh)
("miner")
Order Squamata
Family Anomalepididae

A nonvenomous, burrowing blind snake with tiny, dotlike eyes. Its body was cylindrical with a blunt head and tail that gave it a wormlike appearance.

SIZE About 12 inches (30 cm) long.

FOSSIL HISTORY *Suffosio praedatrix* ("miner huntress") was collected and named by Barbara Standhardt in Big Bend in 1985. It is the oldest blind snake fossil reported so far.

BIG BEND FOSSILS Tiny jaw fragment with one recurved tooth, isolated vertebrae, partial and fragmental vertebrae.

DIET Carnivore. Tiny mammals, reptiles and their eggs, worms, and invertebrates and their larvae.

NATURAL HISTORY *Suffosio praedatrix* spent much of its time underground, as well as beneath logs and moist leaves. Modern blind snakes are parthenogenetic, meaning that adults are all one gender and produce offspring that are essentially clones of the mothers. They are found today in Central and South America. *Suffosio* was likely preyed on by nocturnal digging dinosaurs and mammals.

Quetzalcoatlus northropi
(Ket-zal-Koh-Ah-tel-us)
("Northrop's Aztec feathered serpent god")
Order Pterosauria
Family Azhdarchidae

A giant pterosaur. It had an elongated, stiff neck of almost 6.5 feet (2 meters) in length, unusually long hind legs, and a long, spear-like beak. With eyes that were set in the lower half of the skull, its vision was well developed; the skull likely had some sort of crest, but fossil remains are unclear as to its specific size and shape. The torso was half the length of its head, with a very small tail. The body was covered with hairlike fuzz.

The species had a wingspan of about 36 feet (10.9 meters) with three small fingers (digits); a fourth finger that was 10 times the size of the others supported the wing. The wing membrane was thin like skin, stretching from the first joint of the fourth finger to the pterosaur's forearm, body, and legs. The center of gravity was in the mid-shoulders, which helped the pterosaur manipulate thermal updrafts to soar and glide like a turkey vulture.

SIZE Up to 9 feet (2.75 meters) tall at the shoulder; wingspan up to 36 feet (10.9 meters); estimated weight of 551 pounds (250 kg). The giant size seemed to correlate with the environment along the wide floodplains and river systems.

FOSSIL HISTORY Discovered by Douglas Lawson in 1971, when he found a "long, hollow thin-walled bone"—a wing bone— in Big Bend National Park, under the direction of his professor Wann Langston Jr., Lawson chose the Aztec feathered serpent god, Quetzalcoatl, the creator of Earth and mankind, for the genus name, and the species name referenced John "Jack" Northrop, who designed the Northrop YB-49 fixed-wing bomber in the 1940s, which resembled the pterosaur in flight.

BIG BEND FOSSILS A partial wing of *Q. northopi* consisting of a forelimb with the elongated fourth finger, partial skulls, and

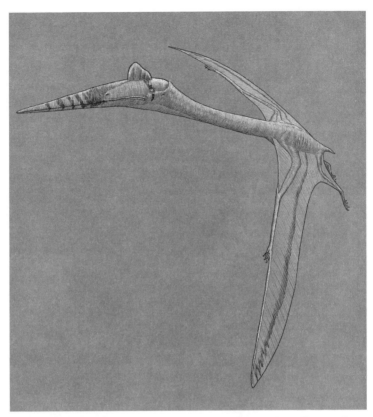

Quetzalcoatlus northropi, as found in Big Bend National Park. This was for a time the largest pterosaur found in North America.

limbs. Collected by Douglas Lawson in 1971; Paul Sereno, Catherine Forster, and Julia Sankey in 1989–1991 and 2000–2007; and Wann Langston Jr. in 1995.

DIET Carnivore. Terrestrial vertebrates like small dinosaurs, lizards, amphibians, and mammals. Waded for fish. May have opportunistically scavenged.

NATURAL HISTORY The nature of its flight remains under debate. Some researchers have suggested that the animal was extremely adept in the air, capable of flight at 80 mph (130 km/h) for 7–10 days at altitudes of 15,000 feet (4,600 meters). Others have suggested that *Quetzalcoatlus* lived more like a bustard or a ground hornbill, able to undertake powered flight but spending most of its time on the ground.

Quetzalcoatlus may have undertaken migrations over immense distances between Europe and North America. Their remains are generally only found inland, however, and it is possible that they spent comparatively little time in the air, functioning instead as largely land-based animals. They were also considered solitary hunters. It has been suggested that they hunted along the rivers and plains like an enormous stork or heron, stalking smaller prey on stiltlike legs and plucking the prey from the shorelines.

There are now two species of *Quetzalcoatlus* in Big Bend.

Quetzalcoatlus lawsoni
(Ket-zal-Koh-Ah-tel-us)
("Lawson's Aztec feathered serpent god")
Order Pterosauria
Family Azhdarchidae

A large pterosaur, about half the size of its giant relative, *Q. northropi*. In 1972, Douglas Lawson and Wann Langston Jr. discovered another site in the Pterodactyl Ridge, where they excavated the remains of three smaller *Quetzalcoatlus* individuals.

SIZE Wingspan almost 15 feet (4.5 meters).

FOSSIL HISTORY The majority of the more than 200 *Q. lawsoni* specimens (including elements from every region of the body) were found in a locality called Pterodactyl Ridge. Collected by Paul Sereno, Catherine Forster, and Julia Sankey in 1989–1991 and 2000–2007, and by Wann Langston Jr. in 1995. This new species was named in honor of Douglas Lawson's discovery of the genus in 1972.

BIG BEND FOSSILS Beak, neck, body, and legs.

DIET Carnivore. Stalked shorelines plucking fish, insects, and small mammals, and scavenging what was left behind by other carnivores.

NATURAL HISTORY Coexisted with *Q. northropi*, living and hunting on land and near rivers and lakes. Waded in groups to prevent being preyed on by crocodilians and dinosaurs. It seems that pterosaurs were more diverse than previously thought.

Wellnhopterus brevirostris
(Well-en-Hop-ter-us Bre-Veer-oh-stris)
("Wellnhofer's short-snouted pterosaur")
Order Pterosauria
Family Azhdarchidae

A medium-sized pterosaur. The beak is rather shorter and proportionally blunter than that of its giant relatives.

SIZE Indeterminate due to lack of clear fossils, but wingspan perhaps 10 feet (3 meters).

FOSSIL HISTORY In 1986, an incomplete pair of jaws and neck vertebrae were discovered in Brewster County. German paleontologist Peter Wellnhofer suggested that they belonged to the then poorly known *Quetzalcoatlus*, which led to a fair amount of confusion. Later paleontologists suggested multiple possible family identities for the animal, including the hatchet-jawed pterosaurs known as thalassodromines. For now, the weight of opinion currently holds that *Wellnhopterus* is likely to be an azhdarchid pterosaur.

In July 2021, the restudied jaws were assigned to another genus and given the name *Javelinadactylus sagebieli* ("Sagebiel's Javelina finger"); in December 2021, the fossils were given the holotype name *Wellnhopterus brevirostris* ("Wellnhofer's short snout"), leaving its official name the subject of some dispute.

BIG BEND FOSSILS Paired jaws, a long bone, and a partially articulated neck. Collected by Douglas Lawson in 1971; Paul Sereno, Catherine Forster, and Julia Sankey in 1989–1991 and 2000–2007; and Wann Langston Jr. in 1995.

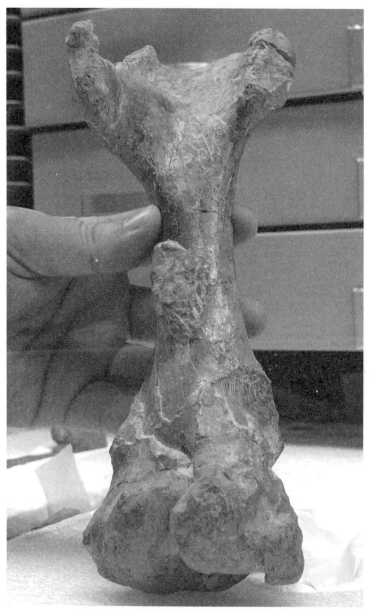

A fossilized humerus of *Quetzalcoatlus lawsoni*. This pterosaur measured about half the size of *Q. northropi*.

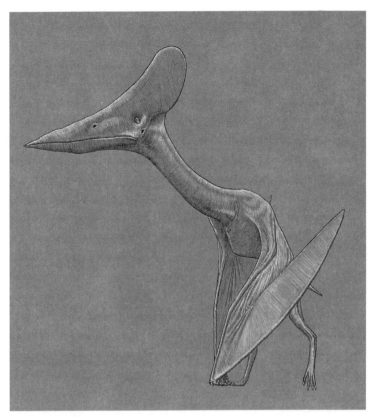

Wellnhopterus brevirostris, a pterosaur about two-thirds the size of *Quetzalcoatlus lawsoni.*

Another eleven species of all different sizes of pterosaurs have been found in Pterodactyl Ridge.

DIET Carnivore. A raptor of prey larger than its body size. Some researchers have suggested that the large, rather blunt beak marks it as a terrestrial hunter, able to tackle relatively large prey, such as cat-sized mammals, dinosaur hatchlings, and large lizards.

NATURAL HISTORY *Wellnhopterus* comes from the same sorts of shallow wetlands and lakeshores as *Q. lawsoni*, but its precise life habits are not known at this time.

Bravoceratops
(Brah-voe-Ser-ah-tops)
("wild horn face")
Order Ornithischia
Family Ceratopsidae

A large chasmosaurine ceratopsian dinosaur, unique to the Big Bend area. It is a stout quadruped, with back legs longer than the front legs. The four short toes end in hooflike claws. Its parrot-beaked skull was topped by two long brow horns (each about 3.3 feet, or 1 meter, long), a shorter nose horn, and hornlets on the cheeks. The 7-foot skull and frill with scalloped edges made up a third of its body length. The snout with a parrot beak was very narrow for the dimensions of the head.

SIZE Up to 28 feet (9 meters) long and 13,000 pounds (about 6,000 kg).

FOSSIL HISTORY *Bravoceratops polyphemus* was named in 2013 from fragmentary material by Steven Wick, a former park paleontological technician who has made many important fossil discoveries and led multiple excavations in the park. The genus name refers to the Rio Bravo, the Mexican name for the Rio Grande; the species is named for the mythical cyclops, in reference to a hollowed area resembling an eye on the top edge of its frill. The genus has been disputed in recent years, and its taxonomic status remains unclear.

BIG BEND FOSSILS Partial adult skull, parts of both brow horns, braincase with the back of skull detached, and eye socket bone.

DIET Herbivore. Possible forage includes ferns, club moss, palms, cycads, and small flowering plants. May have occasionally scavenged.

NATURAL HISTORY *Bravoceratops polyphemus* lived on the floodplains. Like other ceratopsian species, they may have been relatively sociable animals, traveling and nesting in loose herds. The large frills were likely used for social signaling and intimidation of rivals and potential predators. Younger and inexperienced animals may have been prey for theropod dinosaurs and crocodilians, but adults were probably too dangerous to hunt.

Torosaurus
(tor-oh-Sore-rus)
("perforated lizard")
Order Ornithischia
Family Ceratopsidae

A large, somewhat rare chasmosaurine ceratopsid dinosaur. The back legs of this stout quadruped were longer than the front legs. The four short toes ended in hooflike claws. The elongated frill (7 to 9 feet, 2.2–2.8 meters) was twice as wide as it was long and curved upward at the rear. As the animal matured, it developed a circular or oval windowlike opening on either side of the midline bone. Like the related *Triceratops* and *Bravoceratops*, it had a parrot-beaked skull with two long brow horns and a shorter snout horn, as well as small cheek hornlets.

SIZE Up to 29 feet (8–9 meters) long, weighing 8,000–12,000 pounds (3,629–5,443 kg).

FOSSIL HISTORY *Torosaurus utahensis* was named by Othniel Charles Marsh in 1891, with subsequent species being named in the 1970s. *Torosaurus* remains are quite a bit rarer than those of the contemporary *Triceratops;* there is an ongoing debate on whether *Torosaurus* is indeed a separate genus of ceratopsid, or another species of *Triceratops*. More fossil evidence is needed, but meanwhile, the existence of subadult animals currently assigned to *Torosaurus* and genuine differences in anatomy make it likely that *Torosaurus* is its own genus.

BIG BEND FOSSILS Remains of two adults and one juvenile collected by Wann Langston Jr. in 1970 and Douglas Lawson in 1972.

DIET Herbivore. Ferns, cycads, low-growing shrub branches, and other vegetation.

NATURAL HISTORY The relative rarity of *Torosaurus* may suggest competition with *Triceratops* and a more specialized lifestyle or habitat that allowed it to carve out its own niche. The enormous frill was likely an example of sexual selection.

Kritosaurus
(Kree-toh-Sore-us)
("separated lizard")
Order Ornithischia
Family Hadrosauridae

A large hadrosaur with a flat head and prominent nasal crest. The nose was composed of a large tab of bone that extended from the nostrils to above the eyes and then folded in on itself on the forehead. The hind limbs had three toes; the forearms had three hoof-shaped fingers thought to be used for making nests and pulling plants.

SIZE Up to 30 feet (9 meters) long, weighing 5,000 pounds (2,268 kg).

FOSSIL HISTORY Barnum Brown discovered the first *Kritosaurus* fossil in New Mexico in 1904 and named this dinosaur in 1910. In 1940, he discovered a skull and limb bones in Big Bend. For decades, *Kritosaurus* was closely identified with—and believed to be synonymous with—the related and better known *Gryposaurus*, but it is currently considered its own genus.

BIG BEND FOSSILS Skull parts and body skeleton elements were collected by Thomas Lehman, Steven Wick, and Jonathan Wagner in 2016. *Kritosaurus* specimens collected in the Big Bend area have not been assigned a species.

DIET Herbivore. A browser of leaves, ferns, and tender woody material.

NATURAL HISTORY It has been hypothesized that the large nose gave these dinosaurs a keen sense of smell, which allowed them to identify social ranking, sexes, or species. *Kritosaurus* lived in social groups and may have communicated with its fellows through honks or elaborately colored inflatable nose sacs, akin to the throat sacs of frogs. It shared the landscape with several other types of hadrosaurs, including *Angulomastacator* and *Gryposaurus*.

Gryposaurus
(Gripe-oh-Sore-rus)
("hook-nosed lizard")
Order Ornithischia
Family Hadrosauridae

An arch-nosed hadrosaur and one of the most common hadrosaur fossils found in the park. Its prominent nasal arch extends up the head and is rounded in front of the eyes. Like other hadrosaurs, it was capable of moving on two legs or four, and it could rear up to reach food as high as 13 feet (4 meters) above ground. It cropped off plant material with its bill, shaped like a duck's, and ground the plant material with its extensive battery of teeth.

Gryposaurus skin impressions show a hide with scales of many different shapes, including a line of small pyramids along the dorsal area to the end of the tail. On the flank and tail the scales look like limpet shells, and on the neck and sides of the body they were uniform polygons.

SIZE Up to 30 feet (7.6–9 meters) long, weighing between 6,000 and 7,000 pounds (2,700–3,175 kg).

FOSSIL HISTORY Originally named by Canadian paleontologist Lawrence Lambe in 1914, the genus rapidly became one of the better-known American hadrosaurs, with multiple recognized species. The species from the Big Bend area, *Gryposaurus alsatei*, was named after Chief Alsate, the last leader of the Chisos band

A piece of fossilized hadrosaur skin. Fossils of soft tissues such as skin are rare because the tissue will disintegrate if it does not fossilize very quickly. *Photo courtesy of S. Wick; used with permission.*

of Mescalero Apache who lived in the Big Bend region during the 1700s. A rock formation in the park is said to evoke Alsate's profile.

This hadrosaur commingled with *Alamosaurus* and *Quetzalcoatlus*, and the discoverers believed it was also the last hadrosaur to exist before the dinosaur extinction event.

BIG BEND FOSSILS Known from a partial adult skull, vertebrae, and limb bones, as well as fossilized skin impressions, the first known from Big Bend and the second in the state of Texas.

DIET Herbivore. A grazer and browser that ate the branches, leaves, and fruit of conifers and flowering trees from higher levels than other hadrosaurs.

NATURAL HISTORY *Gryposaurus alsatei* likely was an adaptable and successful herding herbivore; it may have had as great an impact on its environment as elephants do on theirs today. The purpose of its nasal arch has been debated. It may have functioned as a butting weapon or for the identification of sexes. The animal's diet may not have been restricted to leafy plants; some hadrosaurs devoured mollusks or the spongy wood from rotting logs.

Alamosaurus
(Al-ah-Moe-Sore-rus)
("cottonwood lizard")
Order Saurischia
Family Saltisauridae

An enormous long-necked dinosaur. *Alamosaurus* was a member of a late-surviving group of sauropods called titanosaurs. It was the largest dinosaur in Cretaceous North America, with a long, heavy neck held at a roughly 45-degree angle, a whiplike tail, and four thick columnar legs. Because the head was extremely small, however, the fossilized skulls remain unknown at this time. Its flanks were partially covered in osteoderms.

The presence of these sauropods in the Cretaceous Black Peaks Formation marks them as among the last nonavian dinosaurs to exist in Big Bend and the world before the extinction event that ended the Cretaceous.

SIZE Up to 80 feet (25 meters) long and up to 65,000 pounds (29,000 kg) or larger.

FOSSIL HISTORY *Alamosaurus sanjuanensis* ("cottonwood lizard from San Juan") was named in 1921 by Charles Whitney

Alamosaurus, one of the last of the long-necked sauropods. It is famous for leaving large caches of fossils, and more of them have been found in Big Bend than anywhere else on the continent.

Gilmore from remains discovered in San Juan County, New Mexico. The name refers to the cottonwood tree, known in Spanish as *alamo*. (That the dinosaur is known from Texas, home of another famous Alamo, is a happy coincidence.) In the following years, *Alamosaurus* remains were found throughout the American Southwest.

In 1940, Barnum Brown, Roland T. Bird, and Erich M. Schlaikjer discovered huge neck vertebrae in Big Bend, which were taken back to the American Museum of Natural History in New York.

Wann Langston Jr. also discovered multiple *Alamosaurus* remains in the years between 1947 and 1973, including an articulated torso and two femurs. In 1997, Dana Biasatti, a graduate student from the University of Texas at Dallas, discovered a bone sticking out of a hill that turned out to be ten articulated neck bones, the smallest of which weighed about 475 pounds (215 kg); it took six men to carry it miles to a truck parked on the nearest road. After moving three more of the vertebrae, the University of Texas at Dallas and the Perot Museum of Nature and Science used a helicopter in 2001 to transport the remaining parts of the dinosaur to the nearest road, where they were trucked to Dallas. This was the first dinosaur airlift in Big Bend National Park. Constructed from these bones, a complete Alamosaurus is on display at the Perot Museum.

BIG BEND FOSSILS Neck and dorsal vertebrae, sacrum, femurs, small blunt cropping teeth, gastroliths, humerus, ulna, and ilium. More *Alamosaurus* fossils have been found in Big Bend than anywhere else in North America so far.

DIET Herbivore. A canopy browser, *Alamosaurus* stripped foliage from the upper branches of trees.

NATURAL HISTORY *Alamosaurus* lived in herds in the warm and dry climate around lakes and river basins between mountains. They laid eggs and, like other titanosaurs, probably nested in large groups for protection of their babies from large carnivores. A fully grown *Alamosaurus* was likely an ecosystem engineer on a scale difficult to imagine today, knocking over trees, digging wells in more arid environments like modern elephants, and reshaping forests and plains with its passage and droppings.

The reappearance of *Alamosaurus* in North America is notable in part because sauropods seemingly disappeared from the continent in the Early Cretaceous, despite persisting elsewhere (called an extirpation, or local extinction). For 35–40 million years, no sauropods seem to have survived in North American ecosystems. It appears, however, that *Alamosaurus* and other sauropods returned to North America by way of South America during the Late Cretaceous along the Isthmus of Panama. Big Bend scientists Thomas Lehman and Alan B. Coulson discovered a unique ball-and-socket joint in titanosaurs from North America and found it to be similar to South American titanosaurs, suggesting that the ancestors of *Alamosaurus* originated in the southern continent.

Tyrannosaurus rex
(Ter-Ran-NO-sore-us)
("king tyrant lizard")
Order Saurischia
Family Tyrannosauridae

An enormous predatory dinosaur. This is the most famous dinosaur in the world and among the best known from the fossil record. *Tyrannosaurus* had a huge bone-crushing skull, a heavy build, two long hind legs, and a heavy tail. Its two-fingered hand was at the end of small but heavily muscled forelimbs.

SIZE Up to 40 feet (12.3 meters) long, 13 feet (3.96 meters) tall at the hips, weighing up to 30,800 pounds (14,000 kg).

FOSSIL HISTORY Discovered in 1900 by Barnum Brown, from a fossil site in eastern Wyoming. *Tyrannosaurus rex* ("king tyrant lizard") was named in 1905 by Henry Fairfield Osborn, director of the American Museum of Natural History. Throughout the twentieth century, more than 50 semicomplete specimens were recovered, including the famed "Sue," an almost complete individual that ended up at the center of a long-running legal battle.

Tyrannosaurus remains are also known from the Javelina Formation. An upper jaw was found by Douglas Lawson, and a tail vertebra and part of a leg were found more recently. In 2014, Steven Wick suggested that there is reason to believe that the remains

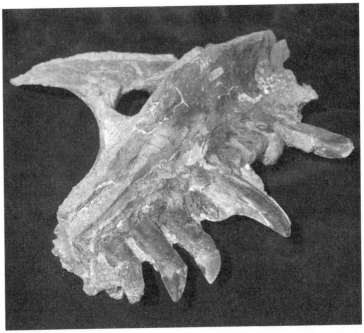

A fossil upper jaw of *Tyrannosaurus rex*. The teeth ranged between 4 and 6 inches long, but they may have been much longer in the gum area.

come from a new species of the genus *Tyrannosaurus*, perhaps one smaller than the tyrannosaurs of Montana and Wyoming. The fossils are not yet distinct enough to determine a new species, and more remains are needed.

BIG BEND FOSSILS A fragment of an upper jaw collected by Douglas Lawson in 1970. The upper tail vertebra of an adult collected by Steven Wick in 2014.

DIET Carnivore. Its diet shifted from small prey when it was young to progressively larger and more powerful prey as it aged.

NATURAL HISTORY Evolving from small dinosaurs not dissimilar to dromaeosaurs, the *Tyrannosaurus* of the latest part of the Cretaceous absolutely dominated the predator guilds of western North America. Younger animals were swift-pursuit predators that squeezed out other species of medium-sized predators; adults were tanks with teeth, able to hunt extraordinarily large prey.

The lifestyle of the Javelina *Tyrannosaurus* is unclear, but the paleobiology of *Tyrannosaurus rex* is fairly well known. Evidence from boneyards and footprints suggests that tyrannosaurs may have been somewhat social animals, but fossils also preserve evidence of crushing bites from other members of the species. Lesions pitting the skulls of *T. rex* show that many also suffered from parasitic infections, perhaps passed along by their habit of biting each other's faces. Despite innumerable films showing tyrannosaurs attacking animals like *Triceratops* head-on, it may have hunted like a modern Komodo dragon, by striking from ambush, inflicting a hideous wound with its powerful jaws, and following the weakening animal until it dropped dead. As do most carnivores, *Tyrannosaurus* both hunted and scavenged as opportunity allowed.

Ptilodus
(Till-oh-Dus)
("soft-haired")
Order Multituberculata
Family Ptilodontidae

Called multituberculates because the teeth of this mammal had many tooth points (tubercules) arranged in rows on each tooth. It had a rodentlike skull with long incisors on the top and bottom jaws. The tail was prehensile, like a monkey's, and the ankle joints allowed the animal to crawl down a tree trunk headfirst like a squirrel.

SIZE Shaped like an average squirrel, but ranging in size from the tiniest mouse to a beaver.

FOSSIL HISTORY The genus was named by Edward Drinker Cope in 1881. Species found in Big Bend were *Ptilodus douglassi*, *P. mediaevus*, and a new species.

The rodentlike *Ptilodus*. This mammal's family has a fossil record spanning 130 million years. It coexisted for a time with the dinosaurs.

BIG BEND FOSSILS An assortment of bumpy teeth collected by Ross Maxwell et al. in 1967 and Judith Schiebout in 1974. In 1986, Barbara Standhardt found and named the new species *Ptilodus torridus* ("parched soft-haired"), after the hot and dry condition of the discovery site.

DIET Omnivore-granivore. Terrestrial tough seeds and plants, broken or sawed through by a massive fourth premolar that was often serrated.

NATURAL HISTORY *Ptilodus* was one of the survivors of the dinosaur extinction that became diverse and abundant in the jungles of the Paleocene. Upwards of 200 species of multituberculates have been found in the fossil localities of the time. Multituberculates existed worldwide in many different niches, from burrowing in the ground to living in trees. They were the longest living group of mammals, though they were subsequently replaced by true rodents. *Ptilodus* peaked in the Paleocene and was extinct by the early Oligocene.

·ᴄ₆ 5 ᴐ᠙·

RIVERS AND ASH

The PALEOGENE BLACK PEAKS, HANNOLD HILL, and the COMBINED FORMATIONS

PALEOGENE BLACK PEAKS FORMATION
Paleocene to Early Eocene
North America Land Mammal Ages (NALMA)
  from 66 Ma (Torrejonian Age) to 56 Ma (Tiffanian Age)
Time Traveler's Field Notes: *60 mya, March 19, 3:00 pm*
200 miles inland of the Western Interior Seaway

THE SWAMP IS SOAKING. THE AFTERNOON RAIN IS WARM AGAINST your face, pattering down in heavy sheets through the verdant canopies. It's afternoon, but the understory is a place of deep and abiding shadows, generations of leaves compacting down into sucking mud. Water lies in black pools around you, the raindrops spreading in concentric circles amid the chirping of frogs. The humidity is almost unbearable, a smothering, suffocating blanket against your skin.

Millions of years have passed since the extinction event, and the world has been reformed. Rain forests that once had open canopies and diverse interactions between insects and plants have taken on a new, more familiar shape, with ranks upon ranks of tall trunks of a few different species shading the forest floor from the sun. There are no massive herbivores left to bulldoze pathways through the trees; the game paths around you are smaller, winding through tangles of brush where fallen timber has let in precious sunlight. This is not a dinosaur forest; it has not been a dinosaur forest for a long, long time.

Look around, however, and you begin to notice signs of the new order. There are wallows in the mud where something has been rooting, and as you crouch to examine it you find long strands of russet fur stuck in the ooze. Out in the swamp, a trio of beasts is swimming across the black water. You raise your binoculars in time to see them clamber out onto a narrow strip of raised earth, shaking their furry bodies. The mother *Titanoides* and her two cubs are stocky, bearlike mammals with long, drooping lips. Leeches are fastened behind the ear of one of the cubs, and as you watch, it yawns and shakes its head, revealing long, tusklike fangs. The mother noses at the cub, blinking. And then, heavily, she and her young splash back into the water.

You and the mother both miss it when it happens. There are two cubs swimming along behind her; then there is a swirl in the water, and one of them has vanished, without even a cry of alarm. You scan the water for a while, waiting for it to reemerge. The mother glances back, notices that one of her cubs is missing. She bleats in alarm and swims back, calling out. But there is no answer, and her other cub is getting tired of treading water. Unhappily, she swims on, and the two of them vanish through the submerged trees.

The crocodile surfaces sometime later, a mound of fur clutched in its jaws. You put the binoculars down, listening to the frogs. It's a new world. But the more things change, sometimes, the more they stay the same.

GEOLOGY OF THE PALEOGENE BLACK PEAKS FORMATION

Despite the extinction event at the end of the Cretaceous, the fundamental geology of the Big Bend landscape did not greatly change. About 3 million years after the extinction, the Paleogene Black Peaks Formation was deposited from the same river system and floodplain that had developed during the Aguja. The uplift of the Rocky Mountains to the west created fault lines, splitting off numerous tributaries from the rivers. This formation's geology stems from river sandstone and overbank mudstone deposits, creating the ancient maroon and black soil layers that alternate through the formation and give it a candy-striped appearance.

The Black Peaks environment was dominated by dense forests of tall trees, cut through by rivers and lakes. There are layers of logjam sandstone where trees line the river channels in a floodplain, resembling a forest standing in water like the Atchafalaya River basin of Louisiana. The trees were undercut by the water through their roots, fell into the ancient river, and followed the flow of the river to where they eventually were buried and petrified by river minerals. There are hundreds of fallen trees in this sandstone deposit.

WHERE TO SEE THE BLACK PEAKS FORMATION

Visit the Fossil Discovery Exhibit overlooking East-Central Tornillo Flat, or walk along the Grapevine Hills Trail.

FOSSIL REMAINS OF THE PALEOGENE BLACK PEAKS FORMATIONPLANTS

The fossils of the logjam sandstone were primarily *Paraphyllanthoxylon abbotti*—flowering dicot trees with more than 40 log diameters that averaged 3.3 feet (1 meter). The largest measured 94 inches (2.4 meters), with a length of almost 33 feet (10 meters). The trees grew in year-round rivers and so had no growth rings from seasonal water stress. Trees found elsewhere in the formation did have tree rings, suggesting seasonal changes away from the river.

The species was named in honor of the first scientist to study this logjam, Dr. Maxine Abbott, who passed away before her work was completed.

Reptiles

With the extinction of the dinosaurs and pterosaurs, the era of massive reptiles passed from Big Bend. The remaining reptiles included crocodilians like *Borealosuchus* and an assortment of lizards, turtles, and snakes.

Small Mammals

Some mammals, like the insectivorous *Mixodectes* ("mixed biter"), originated in the Cretaceous and persisted in Big Bend until the heated thermal maximum occurred between the Paleocene and Eocene (about 55 mya). Other species present include the 4–12 inch (10–30 cm) elephant shrew (*Iluplaletes disceptatrix*, "hidden simple huntress"), a ground-dwelling quadruped with a long scaly rat tail and a tongue that it flicked out like an anteater to pick up insects of all kinds. Also present was *Paleotomus senior* ("older, old part"), an otterlike fish-eater with robust teeth; it weighed 3 pounds (1.4 kg) and survived until the late Eocene (37–34 mya).

Primate Ancestors

After the extinction, primate ancestors from the Family Plesiodapidae ("near *Adapis*") were the first primate fossils found in Big Bend. Plesiadapids resembled squirrels, with narrow, triangular insectivore teeth. These early primates rapidly diversified and became abundant.

The Paleocene Black Peaks Formation has produced numerous fossil teeth, jaws, and skulls from multiple animals in this family, including *Plesiadapis gidleyi* ("Gidley's near Adapis"),

Phenacolemur, an ancestor of lemurs. The size of a squirrel, this mammal lived in the canopy of the forests of ancient Big Bend.

Nannodectes gidleyi ("Gidley's dwarf biter"), *Navajovius kohlhaasae* ("Kohlhaas's primate of the Navajo"), and a species of *Chiromyoides* ("hand similarity"). The Plesiodapidae were present until the early Eocene, when true primates appeared and outcompeted their relatives.

Other primate relatives present in Black Peaks included the fruit- and sap-eating *Phenacolemur frugivorus* ("fruit-eater appearing lemur"), an arboreal ancestor of modern lemurs with robust cheek teeth (for grinding seeds) and a large pair of lower incisors that extended out of its jaw to grasp and manipulate food.

Large Herbivorous Mammals

The extinction of the dinosaurs opened up ecological niches of all sizes with new opportunities for mammals, which diversified rapidly in the millennia after the asteroid strike. The pantodonts ("all teeth") were one of the first mammal groups to develop a large body size, expanding into a diverse array of forms that encompassed everything from big, hippolike animals to smaller arboreal herbivores. Many are known for distinctive, tapirlike teeth, including cheek teeth shaped like the Greek letter lambda (λ). This reference to tooth shape is included in the genus name *Barylambda* and others. Originating in Asia during the middle Paleocene, pantodonts migrated to North America and persisted there until the late Eocene.

Archaic ungulates—formerly known as condylarths—also found success throughout the Paleocene. These hoofed animals started with five hoofed toes, before diversifying into families with either an odd (perissodactyl) or even (artiodactyl) number of toes. They were the largest mammals of the Late Cretaceous and early Paleocene and ate a mainly herbivorous diet.

Archaic ungulates of the Paleogene Black Peaks included phenacodonts ("similar teeth"), sheep-sized animals with a long, stout body, a trunk like a tapir, tusks, and a long tail. These lasted until the middle Eocene and left no modern descendants. Hyopsodonts ("high teeth") were agile, long-bodied relatives of the horse, with very short legs that resembled those of dachshunds. With a large brain, keen sense of smell, and possibly the ability to echolocate, *Hyopsodus* was the last archaic ungulate to go extinct by 36 mya.

Not all archaic ungulates were herbivores. The arctocyonids ("bear doglike") appeared immediately after the extinction event, starting as small predators but reaching the size of wolves by the end of the Paleocene. They had muscular limbs and large canines, and some sported a long, heavy tail. These formidable animals were eventually replaced by new families of carnivorous mammals 50 mya.

Notable Species of the Paleogene Black Peaks Formation

Champsosaurus
(Champ-so-Sore-rus)
("crocodile lizard")
Order Choristodera
Family Champsosauridae

A semiaquatic reptile, resembling but not related to crocodiles. Its snout was elongated, like those of modern gharials, with nose holes on the very tip. It had a relatively long neck; small, sharp, conical teeth; and a set of palatal teeth, like the mosasaurs. Behind its eyes, the muscles in its wide jaw were very large, for a quick, powerful bite.

SIZE Up to 12 feet (3.5 meters) long, weighing 80 pounds (36 kg).

FOSSIL HISTORY Named in 1877 by Edward Drinker Cope from vertebrae found in Montana. Representatives of the genus have been found throughout North America and in Europe.

BIG BEND FOSSILS The most complete *Champsosaurus* skeleton found in southern North America was collected in the Big Bend Paleocene Black Peaks Formation by Kenneth Barnes in 2010, along with loose teeth.

DIET Carnivore. Mostly fish and small animals plucked from the land and water.

NATURAL HISTORY Living in rivers and lakes with slow-moving fresh water, *Champsosaurus* filled an ecological niche similar to that of alligators and crocodiles. Females were able to go on land to lay eggs, but males did not have the hip joints to leave the water. *Champsosaurus* survived the extinction event in Big Bend, and the genus lingered in Wyoming, Colorado, Montana, and Canada until about 63.3 mya. Around the world, some representatives of the family survived into the Miocene.

Borealosuchus
(Bore-ee-Al-oh-Sook-us)
("boreal or northern crocodile")
Order Crocodilia
Clade Eusuchia

A midsized, semiaquatic crocodilian. *Borealosuchus* was closely related to—but not a member of—the family that includes modern alligators and crocodiles. It had a long wedge-shaped head on the body of a modern alligator.

SIZE Up to 9 feet (2.8 meters) long, with a 14-inch (36 cm) skull; weight of around 200 pounds (91 kg).

FOSSIL HISTORY Named in 1997 by Christopher Brochu, a paleontologist specializing in crocodilians. A boreal forest is a northern ecosystem notable for its many conifer trees. These trees were part of the animal's habitat when it existed in the Paleogene Black Peaks. The precise species present in Big Bend remains unclear due to the lack of clear fossil evidence.

BIG BEND FOSSILS An incomplete skull lacking the region behind the eyes, an upper jaw with 33 holes for teeth, part of a lower jaw, and rectangular dorsal osteoderms. Remains collected by Jack Wilson, Malcolm C. McKenna, and George Whitaker in 1952 and 1962–1963.

DIET Carnivore. Small mammals, reptiles, smaller crocodilians, and fish.

NATURAL HISTORY *Borealosuchus* lived in swampy, overgrown forests and floodplains that held water from prolonged wet periods. Big Bend was the most southern occurrence of this extinct crocodilian, and it lingered on into the Canoe Formation, 46 mya.

Bottosaurus
(Boe-toe-Sore-rus)
("Botto's lizard")
Clade Eusuchia
Family Alligatoridae

A caiman with a blunt snout and a robust jaw. Its front teeth each had three cusps, while its back teeth were more typical of a crocodile. The bony osteoderms covering its body were unusually thick.

SIZE Fossil evidence is too scrappy to assign a maximum size, but it may have grown as large as a modern caiman, up to 88 pounds (40 kg).

FOSSIL HISTORY Originally named by paleontologist Louis Agassiz in 1849, and a few different species have been recorded over the ensuing century and a half. Adam Cossette and Christopher Brochu introduced the species in 2018 from the Black Peaks Formation as the first known fossil species of caiman in western North America. The majority are found in the eastern United States. The species *B. fustidens* ("Botto's club-tooth lizard") is notable for its globe-shaped teeth adapted to crushing shells of bivalves.

BIG BEND FOSSILS Remains of a partial skull and skeleton were collected by Jack Wilson, Malcolm McKenna, and George Whitaker in 1952 and 1962–1963, and Jack Wilson in 1969.

DIET Carnivore. Its teeth suggest that it was a specialized shell cracker, devouring turtles, smaller crocodilians and juveniles of its own species, as well as fish of all kinds.

NATURAL HISTORY A resident of a semitropical to tropical forest environment with lakes and meandering rivers. Larger adults were relatively safe from predation, but the youngsters had to watch out for large fish, birds, mammals, and their own relatives. *Bottosaurus fustidens* went extinct about 55 mya when the climate heated up substantially.

Barylambda jackwilsoni
(Bear-ree-Lam-dah)
("Jack Wilson's heavy lambda teeth")
Order Cimolesta
Family Barylambdidae

A large, stocky herbivorous pantodont mammal. It had a robust skeleton and tail, powerful limbs, hooflike toes, and long claws.

SIZE Up to 8 feet (2.5 meters) long, weighing 1,430 pounds (650 kg).

FOSSIL HISTORY The genus *Barylambda* was originally described from teeth in 1937. This species was named in 1974 by Judith Schiebout to honor her mentor, Jack Wilson. Somewhat smaller than other species of its genus, it is also sometimes synonymized with the pantodont *Caenolambda jepseni* ("Jepsen's new lambda tooth"). *Caenolambda pattersoni* was also a noted Big Bend species.

BIG BEND FOSSILS Teeth, jawbones, partial skull, and limb bones collected by Jack Wilson, Malcolm McKenna, and George Whitaker in 1952 and 1962–1963.

DIET Herbivore. A generalist browser of soft leaves, young branches, and berries.

NATURAL HISTORY *Barylambda* may have used its sturdy tail like a tripod to reach high vegetation, pulling it down with large slothlike claws. With a body size between a mastiff and a rhinoceros, this pantodont would have been almost invincible to land predators of its time. *Barylambda* and *Caenolambda* were successful browsers, lingering until climatic changes caused their preferred forests to transition into grassland. Both subsequently vanished.

Titanoides
(Tie-tan-Noy-deez)
("titanlike")
Order Cimolesta
Family Titanoideidae

A large, bearlike pantodont mammal. It had a stocky body; a broad, robust head and snout; and large, muscular limbs with five strong claws on each foot. Males had downward-pointing saber-like tusks in the upper jaw.

SIZE Up to 10 feet (3 meters) long, weighing 330 pounds (150 kg).

Titanoides, the largest swampland herbivore in its habitat. It had long canines and sharp bearlike claws. Fossils have been found as far north as Alberta, Canada.

FOSSIL HISTORY *Titanoides* was originally named from Canadian remains in 1917. The species *T. zeuxis* ("linking titanlike") was collected and named by then-graduate student Judith Schiebout, who later stated that this pantodont was the best find of her career. Other species found with *Titanoides zeuxis* were *T. molestus* ("troublesome titanlike") and *T. gidleyi* ("Gidley's titanlike"), which existed in the later Hannold Hill Formation as well.

BIG BEND FOSSILS An almost complete skull with no tusks, suggesting it was female.

DIET Herbivore. A browser of leaves, fruit, and underwater vegetation.

NATURAL HISTORY *Titanoides* lived in the tropical swamps, using their tusks to root through tough vegetation. During the mating season, males likely engaged in spectacular battles over territory and females. Such tusks on a semiaquatic animal may have been accompanied by thick layers of fat, as seen on modern hippos and tapirs, which could have insulated the animals from each other's tusks.

Psittacotherium
(sit-Tak-oh-Theer-ee-um)
("parrot beast")
Order Cimolesta
Family Stylinodontidae

A medium-sized nonplacental mammal. *Psittacotherium* had a large skull with massive short, deep jaws and a parrotlike snout. Those jaws contained three types of teeth: chisel-like front teeth with an orange ribbon of enamel on the front to keep the edges sharp, prominent canine tusks for gnawing and rooting, and grinding teeth with a distinct pattern not seen in any other mammal. Its skull showed areas of muscle attachment for a large and well-developed tongue. Its powerful front limbs were highly specialized for digging, with large, five-digit, heavy claws on each foot.

SIZE Up to 3.5 feet (1.1 meters) long, weighing 110 pounds (50 kg).

FOSSIL HISTORY The genus was named by Edward Drinker Cope in 1882. The species name *multifragum* ("many fragments") refers to the many tooth fragments found. *Psittacotherium* belongs to a mysterious group of mammals called the Cimolesta, a sister group of the marsupials and placental mammals alive today.

BIG BEND FOSSILS Skull and jaw fragments, canine teeth, molars, and incisors found by Judith Schiebout and her dad, Joe, in 1974.

DIET Omnivore. Tubers, carrion, vegetation.

NATURAL HISTORY The genus originated in North America, was not very diverse, and has no known surviving descendants. Based on the teeth, its diet seems to have been rather varied; it may have subsisted on roots, tubers, and carrion, rather like a large armadillo.

Periptychus
(per-Rip-tee-kus)
("surrounding fold")
Order Condylarthra
Family Periptychidae

A small, archaic hoofed mammal known primarily for its distinctive teeth. Members of this family generally had a robust skeleton with a sturdy tail; the skull was flat and broad-faced, with a small braincase and a moderately long snout. Each foot had five hoofed digits of equal size.

SIZE Sheep-sized, around 44 pounds (20 kg).

FOSSIL HISTORY The genus was named by Edward Drinker Cope in 1882, but at the time he gave no explanation of the origin of the Latin name. *Periptychus carinidens* ("surrounding fold keeled tooth") is an index fossil that represents the beginning of the Torrejonian Land Mammal Age. Its deep jaws and crenulated teeth with vertical striations were unusual and efficient for grinding tough plant material. The teeth are found throughout North America and suggest that the family was widespread and successful. The species *P. carinidens* and *P. superstes* ("survivor of surrounding fold") were found in the Big Bend area.

BIG BEND FOSSILS Assorted teeth collected by Ross Maxwell et al. in 1967 and Barbara Standhardt in 1986.

DIET Herbivore. Sabal palms, conifers, and flowering bushes.

NATURAL HISTORY No mammal with a similar suite of traits exists today. All that can be said is that *Periptychus* was a ground-dwelling generalist, possibly a digger, and an herbivore well adapted to crushing plant material with its unusual teeth. The family contains large animals with robust skeletons as well as smaller ones. They were likely preyed on by larger mammalian carnivores and crocodilians.

Phenacodus
(Fee-nah-Koh-duss)
("deceiver's tooth")
Order Perissodactyla
Family Phenacodontidae

A heavily built mammal. *Phenacodus* was one of the earliest groups of hoofed animals. It had an elongated narrow skull, long legs, five complete hoofed toes, and a long powerful tail. Its teeth had simple rounded cusps. It also had canine tusks, which were longer in males than in females. It may have had either a short trunk or a prehensile lip, like a tapir.

SIZE Ranged from the size of a domestic cat to that of modern sheep.

FOSSIL HISTORY Phenacodonts were among the most common fossils found in North America in the mid-Paleocene. Named by Edward Drinker Cope in 1873, the genus is represented by multiple species of various sizes, from the small *Phenacodus gid-*

Phenacodus, a hoofed mammal with possible woodland camouflage. It ate everything it could find in its forests.

leyi, *P. bisonensis*, and *P. matthewi* to *P. grangeri*, the largest family member. All species were known from Big Bend, but *P. bisonensis* was part of the first Big Bend fossil exhibit, which featured actual fossils locked in the rock of Tornillo Flat.

BIG BEND FOSSILS Upper and lower jaws with attached and isolated teeth and fragments collected by Ross Maxwell et al. in 1967, Judith Schiebout in 1974, Jill A. Hartnell in 1980, and Barbara Standhardt in 1986.

DIET Omnivore. Fruit, flowering plants, tender leaves, carrion, and small vertebrates.

NATURAL HISTORY One of the earliest and most primitive known ungulates, *Phenacodus* lived on the edge of the woods and was possibly mottled in pigmentation, providing camouflage in its surroundings. Like many animals in the millennia after the Cretaceous extinction, it may have been a generalist browser and omnivore, able to dig and run with equal ease. It lasted until 46 mya, making it one of the latest surviving archaic ungulates.

Chriacus baldwini
(cry-Ak-us)
("Baldwin's useful thing")
Order Arctocyonia
Family Arctocyonidae

A small archaic hoofed mammal, with a lightly built body and long face resembling a living coati. It was an agile tree climber with a long, bony (and possibly prehensile) tail. With flexible, sturdy leg and ankle joints, it could go down a tree headfirst like a modern squirrel. It had five-toed feet and long, curved claws used to dig in the ground and to climb trees.

SIZE Up to 3 feet (1 meter) long, weighing 15 pounds (7 kg).

FOSSIL HISTORY Edward Drinker Cope gave the genus its somewhat mysterious name in 1883. *Chriacus baldwini*, the Big Bend representative of the genus, is named after David Baldwin, who collected one of the first specimens in the area.

BIG BEND FOSSILS Molars collected by Judith Schiebout in 1974.

DIET Omnivore. Insects, fruit, eggs, and small mammals.

NATURAL HISTORY Lived and hunted in the forest canopy and at ground level. The animals were not able to run fast, but the ability to climb trees gave them an advantage against most larger carnivores. They likely had a stronger sense of smell than sight.

Arctocyon
(Ark-toe-Sigh-on)
("bear-dog")
Order Arctocyonia
Family Arctocyonidae

A large, predatory archaic hoofed mammal. It resembled a large wolf with a rounded bearlike body and a long catlike tail. Despite the name, it was not related to bears, dogs, or the "bear dogs," which appeared millennia later.

Arctocyon, a primitive hoofed predator. It is one of 20 genera that had big sharp teeth but no specialized hunting adaptations.

SIZE Up to 4 feet (1.3 meters) long, weighing 130 pounds (60 kg).

FOSSIL HISTORY Named by French paleontologist Henri Marie Ducrotay de Blainville in 1841. The mix of traits and multiple species in this genus has been a source of confusion for paleontologists ever since. Two species are known from Big Bend: *Arctocyon ferox* ("fierce bear-dog") and *A. acrogenius* ("high natural-ability bear-dog").

BIG BEND FOSSILS Low-crowned teeth and jaw fragments collected by Judith Schiebout in 1974.

DIET Omnivore. Large canine tusks and sharper cheek teeth were common to most hoofed mammals. These teeth allowed it to eat meat and plants from the ground.

NATURAL HISTORY *Arctocyon*, the largest genus in the family, lived in the forests of the Big Bend area during a time of extended environmental upheaval. It likely lived like a modern black bear, devouring plants, turning over logs for insects, and mustering surprising turns of speed to hunt smaller prey. Although not particularly swift, younger animals may have been able to climb trees. It walked on the flat of its feet like a bear, rather than on its toes like a wolf.

HANNOLD HILL FORMATION
Early Eocene
NALMA
*from 56 Ma (Clarkforkian Age, mostly eroded) to 50 Ma
(Wasatchian Age)*

GEOLOGY OF THE HANNOLD HILL FORMATION

As the western part of the continent continued to be forced upward by the growing Rocky Mountains, the still, swampy lowlands began to drain out, replaced by steeper, sandier, and faster-flowing rivers. This is the Hannold Hill Formation, a thin and badly eroded set of deposits mostly confined to one area of the park. These rocks coincide with the Paleocene-Eocene Thermal Maximum, a period of extreme global heat that lasted anywhere from 20,000 to 50,000 years. Fed by outpourings of volcanism that dumped huge amounts of carbon dioxide into the air, global temperatures jumped a staggering 41–46°F (5–8°C). Tropical rain forests spread across multiple continents, and representatives of modern families—including horses, camels, rhinoceroses, and true primates—appeared for the first time.

Sadly for our time travel experiment, the Hannold Hill Formation preserves little of those changes. With the oldest strata from an ancient river system, the Exhibit Ridge sandstone member is named for an outcrop that has held various fossil exhibits, including the current one. The middle stratum, the lower mudstone member, exhibits different colors of mudstone from ancient overbank river flooding. The youngest, the upper sandstone member, is from an inland floodplain environment where the sandstone and conglomerate—rounded river rocks of all sizes—came from the swift, flood-prone waterways on the plains.

WHERE TO SEE THE HANNOLD HILL FORMATION

The majority of Hannold Hill is contained on Tornillo Flat in the park, and the Fossil Discovery Exhibit is built on an outcrop of this formation.

FOSSIL REMAINS OF THE HANNOLD HILL FORMATION

Several vertebrates from the Paleocene Black Peaks still existed when Hannold Hill was deposited. These include the primate *Phenacolemur*, the alligator *Borealosuchus*, and the pantodont *Caenolambda*. Poor preservation of much of the site, however, has left its larger biodiversity somewhat unclear.

True Ungulates

As the Paleocene-Eocene Thermal Maximum smothered the world in a blanket of wet heat, hoofed herbivores—the true ungulates—arose and diversified in separate directions. Their ancestors all had five toes, like most mammals, but the pressure of evolution and the availability of open niches pushed early ungulates in multiple directions. Animals that became heavier required feet that could support their weight; animals that prioritized speed needed feet that made them more agile. Unneeded toes became smaller, and often eventually disappeared.

Broadly speaking, two large groups of modern ungulates appeared in the Eocene. The most familiar of them, the artiodactyls ("even-toed"), have cloven hooves made of keratin, the material in human fingernails. Modern members of this family represent an astonishingly diverse range of animals. Along with the more familiar animals, such as pigs, cattle, sheep, and antelope, artiodactyls also include camels, giraffes, llamas, hippopotami, and peccaries (such as javelinas). Whales, which originated from relatives of the hippopotamus at the beginning of the Eocene, are also included in this group.

Animals in another group, the perissodactyls ("odd-toed"), have an odd number of toes—anywhere from one to five. This group includes horses, tapirs, rhinos, and the extinct brontotheres.

Notable Species of the Hannold Hill Formation

Coryphodon
(Core-Iff-fah-don)
("peaked teeth")
Order Cimolesta
Family Coryphodontidae

A large pantodont similar to a hippo. It had a thick body, short robust limbs, a stocky head with a muscular neck, and a broad muzzle with protruding canine tusks. The skull and mandibles also had the rounded jaw flare of a hippopotamus.

SIZE Up to 8 feet (2.4 meters) long and 1,500 pounds (700 kg).

FOSSIL HISTORY Known from multiple species, *Coryphodon* was named in 1845 by English paleontologist Sir Richard Owen, the anatomist who named Dinosauria. *Coryphodon molestus* ("troublesome peaked tooth") is the only species currently known from Big Bend.

BIG BEND FOSSILS Jack Wilson, Malcolm McKenna, and George Whitaker collected two complete skulls, three mandibles, very large canines, shovel-like incisors, and peaked cheek teeth in 1952 and 1962–1963.

DIET Herbivore. Leaves, fruit, flowers, and fungi in the remaining swamps of Big Bend.

NATURAL HISTORY *Coryphodon* migrated to North America from Asia, replacing previous pandodonts like *Barylambda* and *Caenolambda*. A Big Bend quarry record lists remains from multiple individuals, but it is not clear why the animals died together and whether they habitually traveled in groups. A *Coryphodon* individual likely spent a large part of its day in the water and used its tusks to root up plants. As one of the largest mammals of its time, with a brain of only 3.2 ounces (90 g), *Coryphodon* had one of the smallest brain/body ratios in animals living or extinct. Its

Pantodont
Coryphodon molestus
Skull
Eocene
Brewster County, Texas
TMM 40143-12

A fossil *Coryphodon* skull. On the right are what is left of the upper tusks used to uproot plants in its swampy environment. The large sagittal crest on the top of the skull held large muscles for chewing tough vegetation.

enormous size and ability to escape predators in the water put it out of reach for contemporary predators.

Hyracotherium
(Hi-Rak-oh-Theer-ee-um)
("hyraxlike beast")
Order Perissodactyla
Family Paleotheriidae

Really a palaeothere ("ancient beast"), not a horse at all. *Hyracotherium* existed 47–38 mya. It had a vaguely horselike skull and a short snout. Its robust body had forelimbs that were longer than the hind limbs, with four toes (not hooves) on each front foot and three toes on each back foot.

The horse ancestor *Hyracotherium*. The size of a dog, it looked more like a tapir. Fossils of it were among the first Big Bend exhibits.

This small ancestor of the horse roamed the undergrowth of the dense forest foraging for food, and its proportionately larger brain gave it a sensory advantage for watching, smelling, and listening for predators.

SIZE About 14–15 inches (36–38 cm) long, height about 12 inches (30 cm) at the shoulder, the size and weight of a fox terrier.

FOSSIL HISTORY Named in 1841 by Sir Richard Owen for its hyraxlike teeth, as the skeletal remains were scant. *Eohippus* ("dawn horse") was named by Edward Drinker Cope in 1875 as the dawning species of horse history. In 1932, a researcher suggested that they were similar enough for the two genera to be combined. *Hyracotherium* was named 34 years before *Eohippus*, so its name would take precedence. *Eohippus* is still controversial in that some scientists suggest it is not a distinct genus.

"Dawn horses," such as *Hyracotherium augustidens* of the

Black Peaks Formation and *H. vasacciense* of the Hannold Hill Formation, were some of the first horse ancestors that existed after the dinosaur extinction through to the early Eocene.

BIG BEND FOSSILS Mandible fragments with molars—still in the original rock—were on display at the first fossil exhibit in Big Bend National Park.

DIET Herbivore. With low-crowned cheek teeth, it browsed soft leaves, fruits, and berries from the abundance of the tropical Paleocene and Eocene forests.

NATURAL HISTORY A swift little woodland creature adapted to the hothouse world of the Eocene. It was also likely a favored prey item for bone-crushing predatory mammals, primitive carnivores, and mustelids. It vanished toward the end of the Eocene, as the climate began to cool and forests were lost to grasslands. Also, migrations from Asia included fierce predators better adapted to the cold.

THE COMBINED FORMATIONS OF CANOE, CHISOS, AND DEVIL'S GRAVEYARD

Middle to Late Eocene

NALMA

from 50 Ma (Bridgerian Age) to 37 Ma (Chadronian Age)

Time Traveler's Field Notes: *38 mya, February 4, 9 am*

400 miles from the Gulf of Mexico

BROAD-LEAVED TREES SIGH IN THE MORNING BREEZE. SPECKS OF dew linger on the grass. You are standing in a stretch of open, wooded hillside, the morning air humid and cool against your face. The light breeze carries faint notes of ash and pungent gas. Grasshoppers scream in high, plaintive notes from the bracken around you.

Below, the slope levels out into a patchwork plain of verdant, broad-leaved trees and green-gold meadowland, before rising again in an enormous, bulging mountain that broods against the sky. This is the Chisos supervolcano, born from the last great upthrust of the Rocky Mountains, a force of fire and pyroclastic ash on a nearly unimaginable scale. For thousands of years at a time, forests grow on its slopes and crown, waxing tall and lush on volcanic soils. For thousands of years at a time, the mountain sleeps, one more feature of the landscape.

In its shadow, life goes on. A group of enormous, humped titanotheres—club-horned, rhinolike beasts the size of an elephant—browse the forest verge, rumbling to one another, followed by flocks of small birds that snap up the insects they disturb with their browsing. Bands of horselike animals traverse the open plain beyond, heads bobbing up to check for danger in between mouthfuls of fern and grass. They belong to a hyracodon rhinoceros herd, often called "running rhinos," a group that later in Asia will give rise to the largest land mammals that have ever existed.

Here, they are swift-running, sharp-eyed herbivores, alert to the presence of danger.

As you watch, one band of hyracodon drifts to a halt, perhaps alerted by a warning snort by one of its members. Their striped heads pop up, surveying their surroundings. Through your binoculars, you see their tails begin to swish in nervous arcs. A burly, long-jawed shape loping toward them on the plain is a mesonychid, a carnivore about the size of a bear. Its body is camouflaged in a complex pattern of spots and blotches. If it manages to catch them by surprise, its powerful jaws and hooked teeth are capable of bringing down one of the hyracodon herd. But this one is approaching openly, ignoring the unhappy rhinos. It trots by them on hooflike paws, headed off on some unknowable errand. As it passes, the rhinos visibly relax, ears flicking, and begin once more to graze.

But they have misjudged the source of the danger. You feel it before quite realizing it, a slight tremor in the ground, like a shudder racing over the skin of a sleeping giant. The song of the birds and insects goes quiet. Another tremor, more violent, rocks the ground, and you stumble. Out on the plain, the hyracodon rhinos crouch instinctively. The titanotheres look around, tossing their club-horned heads.

For a moment all is eerie stillness. The world holds its breath. You wait, nerves tingling, watching the mountain, but nothing more happens. For today, at least, the supervolcano remains asleep.

It will not sleep for long.

GEOLOGY OF THE COMBINED FORMATIONS

In the 15 million years between the middle Eocene and the early Oligocene, three different formations were deposited around the same time in the Big Bend area: the Canoe, the Chisos, and the Devil's Graveyard. These formations are defined through the simultaneous deposition of river water and volcanic fire, as the mountain-building west of Big Bend finally gave rise to explosive volcanism within it.

The Canoe Formation was deposited on top of the eroded Hannold Hill Formation by braided river systems. They left massive conglomerate sandstones called the Big Yellow sandstone, along with the red, purple, gray, and maroon mudstones. Gray and white tuff—rocks made of volcanic ash—and basaltic lava are part of this formation. The river corridor was lined with conifers, flowering trees, and plants, and many animals were fossilized around the rivers and lakes.

The Chisos Formation was deposited when the rivers of the time collected the rocks and ash from the onset of volcanic activity. Whatever fossils had been there were often destroyed by lava and hot ash. A few of the fossils found in this formation are *Miocyon*, a small tree-dwelling carnivore; *Epihippus*, a true horse ancestor; and *Menodus*, a brontothere. The beautiful Chisos Mountains were created from an active volcano during this time period.

Finally, the Devil's Graveyard Formation was deposited with volcanic lava and ash in the same river system as the Canoe and Chisos Formations, though its outcrops are found outside the borders of the park. This formation was farther away from active volcanoes in the modern Big Bend, and plentiful fossil remains— mostly teeth—are preserved in its rock. The Devil's Graveyard Formation got its name from James Stevens, a geologist, and paleontologists Margaret Stevens and Jack Wilson in 1984; the name is due in part to the eeriness of the area where the fossil animals were buried.

The animals found in these formations were roughly the same. Turtles and crocodilians inhabited the braided rivers, while mammals of all sizes and shapes flourished in and under the ancient tree canopy. Archaic ungulates like the dachshund-sized *Hyopsodus* and the pantodont *Coryphodon* lingered into the combined formations as well.

WHERE TO SEE THE COMBINED FORMATIONS

The remnants of this period can be seen inside the park around the bulk of the beautiful Chisos Mountains. Hike the South Rim of the Chisos to look down at the Sierra Quemada, the "burned mountains," or check out the colorful layers of volcanic ash and lava around Pine Canyon, Burro Mesa, and Castolon.

FOSSIL REMAINS OF THE COMBINED FORMATIONS

Reptiles

Few fossils of lizards, snakes, and turtles are known from these formations, but some have been preserved. One rather extraordinary land crocodile, *Boverisuchus*, has been recorded.

Rhinoceros

Within the larger perissodactyl family, one living and two extinct families of rhinoceros have made their mark in history. Hyracodonts—the "running rhinos"—belonged to a hornless family with long, horselike bodies and legs. The hornless amynodonts were semiaquatic and hippolike, with large stout bodies, big gaping mouths, and huge canines. These two families first appeared from Asia in the middle Eocene and went extinct during the late Oligocene. Finally, the Rhinocerotidae—the modern true rhinoceros we know and love—have horns and thick skin. They lived in North America, Europe, and Asia before they lived in Africa.

All rhinoceros species, living and extinct, have cheek teeth with connected crests that look like the Greek letter pi (π), perfect for grinding tough grasses.

Horses

Horses evolved from perissodactyl ancestors at the beginning of the Eocene. The earliest members of the family had four toes on the front feet and three toes on the back feet, like a tapir. Over time, the middle toe lengthened and the side toes became shorter, until

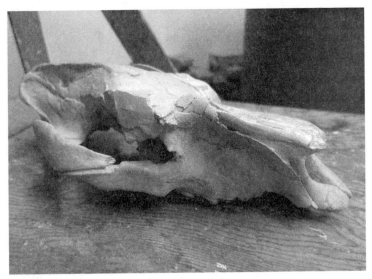

Fossil skull of an undetermined ancestor of the modern rhinoceros. It contained unusual molars with enamel spanning two roots per tooth.

surviving horses were left with one toe on each foot. Their teeth—which at first had short crowns to browse soft leaves—gradually acquired longer crowns, with cementum covering the enamel to help process fibrous grasses.

Brontotheres

Brontotheres were perissodactyls with a large clublike horn on the nose. They were called "thunder beasts" because it was imagined that when these enormous animals ran in a herd, it sounded like thunder. Their earliest relatives were the size of an average dog, but they had grown into giants by the end of the Eocene, with the largest species reaching the size of a modern elephant. They were the last giant mammals in North America until the arrival of mammoths during the frigid Pleistocene Epoch. (This tendency toward large sizes is immortalized in one of the family's other names, titanotheres, or "titan beasts.")

In Big Bend, they are known largely from primitive bronto-theres like *Protitanotherium emarginatum*. Teeth from a larger species, *Duchesneodus uintaensis*, are also known from the area.

Predatory Ungulates

The role of large carnivores in North America was initially played by two separate groups of artiodactyls. The first were the mesony-chids ("middle claws"), a group of artiodactyls with four hoofed digits on each foot. The axis of strength was between the third and fourth toes, or "middle claws," which made for more efficient running. The animals were called "wolves with hooves," and they were scavengers as well as carnivores. Their teeth were heavily worn from regularly cracking bones. The family evolved in Asia in the early Paleocene and migrated over the Beringia land bridge to North America, becoming larger and more predatory before going extinct in the mid-Eocene.

Another family of predatory ungulates included the entelo-donts ("perfect teeth"), a group of rather hoglike predators often referred to as "hell pigs." They were more closely related to hip-pos and whales. Appearing in the late Eocene, these swift, long-jawed omnivores soon grew to truly fearsome sizes, and by the Miocene some members of the family had become the largest animals in their ecosystems. Entelodonts were just as capable at cracking bone as they were at browsing for vegetation. One early member of the family, *Archaeotherium*, is known from Big Bend.

Hyaenodonts

This group of predatory mammals had teeth structures similar to those of hyenas and was distantly related to modern predatory mammals. Hyaenodonts belonged to a family called creodonts ("creative teeth"), the first mammals to evolve a more familiar predatory lifestyle. Their delicate bodies came in a variety of sizes, with slender legs for running and jumping. Their teeth were excellent for shearing meat but so-so for chewing; unlike cats, which can rotate their paws inward, creodonts relied largely on their jaws to catch and dispatch prey.

In the absence of competition from mesonychids, the hyaenodonts followed their evolutionary trajectory, growing larger and dominating the predatory niche for around 26 million years. The family went extinct in the late Miocene.

Primates

Primates of this time included primitive relatives of today's tarsiers, tree-living, prehensile-tailed animals with large brains and forward-facing, predatory eyes. These species included the 16-ounce (454 g) nocturnal *Ourayia uintaensis* (named for Ouray, Colorado, and the Uinta Mountains); the diurnal, small-eyed, 18-ounce (510 g) *Rooneyia viejaensis* ("belonging to the Vieja area of Big Bend"); and the impeccably named *Diablomomys dalquesti* ("Dalquest's tarsier of the Devil's Graveyard Formation"), known only from the Big Bend area and named after the Dalquest family, who owned the property where the fossil was found.

The forests of the combined formations also included relatives of modern lemurs and bushbabies, which are larger diurnal primates with small eyes, a long snout, a great sense of smell, flattened nails instead of claws, and a prehensile tail. These animals were herbivores and insectivores. They included *Mescalerolemur horneri* ("Horner's lemur of the Mescalero Apache"), whose name references both the tribe that inhabited Big Bend from the eighteenth and nineteenth centuries and Norman Horner, a professor at Midwestern State University who worked on primates in Big Bend.

Also present was *Mahgarita stevensi*, a species of lemurlike primate known only from Big Bend. The name refers to Margaret Stevens, who found the skull and teeth of this primate along with many other animals in the Cenozoic deposits of Big Bend.

A tiny skull *(left)* and upper jaw *(right)* belonging to a young adult primate, *Rooneyia*, an ancestor of the living mouse lemur. The skull is the most noted discovery of Jack Wilson.

Notable Species of the Canoe, Chisos, and Devil's Graveyard Formations

Boverisuchus
(Boe-Vair-ih-Sook-us)
("hoofed crocodile")
Clade Eusuchia
Family Planocraniidae

A medium-sized land crocodilian. With long legs and hooflike toes, it walked on the tips of its toes like deer and was able to gallop after its prey. As on other crocodiles, armor plates locked tightly around its body, limbs, and tail. Its skull was high and narrow, with a long, flat snout packed with sharp, serrated teeth. It had an alligatorlike overbite and, in its upper jaw, the characteristic notch found in modern crocodiles.

Boverisuchus. Imagine an alligator that can gallop almost as fast as you can run.

SIZE Up to 10 feet (3 meters) long.

FOSSIL HISTORY Although the genus *Boverisuchus* was named by paleontologist Oskar Kuhn in 1938 from German remains, the species *Boverisuchus vorax* ("insatiable hoofed crocodile") was originally identified with the now dubious genus *Pristichampsus.* Teeth from these animals were at one point mistaken for those of theropods, leading some paleontologists to suggest the survival of nonavian dinosaurs after the Cretaceous extinction.

BIG BEND FOSSILS Osteoderms and teeth fossils were found in the Devil's Graveyard Formation by Margaret Stevens, James Stevens, and Jack Wilson in 1984.

DIET Carnivore. A pursuit predator of terrestrial mammals.

NATURAL HISTORY A throwback to lineages of terrestrial crocodiles common in the Mesozoic Era, *Boverisuchus* likely competed with mammalian carnivores like hyaenodonts and hell pigs.

With a round, dinosaur-like tail and the ability to gallop, it could catch even relatively swift prey. Some modern crocodilians, like the spectacled caiman, are surprisingly comfortable on land and occasionally hunt terrestrially as well.

Stylinodon
(sty-Line-oh-Don)
("pillar teeth")
Order Cimolesta
Family Stylinodontidae

A large, bearlike mammal. Its canine teeth evolved into large chisel-like incisors with the characteristic taeniodont ribbon of self-sharpening orange enamel. It had a blunt-faced skull with a very short snout and a stocky, powerful build.

SIZE Up to 5.7 feet (1.7 meters) long and 242 pounds (80–110 kg).

FOSSIL HISTORY Originally named by Othniel Charles Marsh in 1874. Fossil remains from Big Bend are not conclusive enough to assign a species.

Stylinodon, an inhabitant of arid climates. Its fossils are rare.

BIG BEND FOSSILS A mandible with teeth found in the Devil's Graveyard Formation by Margaret Stevens, James Stevens, and Jack Wilson in 1984.

DIET Herbivore. A grazer and browser of grasses, tender branches, leaves, and fruit.

NATURAL HISTORY *Stylinodon* was the largest and best-known of the taeniodonts, a sister group to placental mammals that appeared in the Paleocene and thrived for about 45 million years. Although its front limbs were strong and muscular, tipped with curving claws, it seems to have been less of a digger than its earlier relative, *Psittacotherium*. It may have used its claws to pull down branches, like a ground sloth. The high-crowned molars covered in enamel continued to grow throughout the animal's life, suggesting a possible grassy diet. Its stocky frame and large claws may have made it a formidable adversary.

Harpagolestes
(har-Pag-oh-Less-teez)
("hooked robber")
Order Perissodactyla
Family Mesonychidae

A large, hoofed ungulate predator the size of a bear. *Harpagolestes* was a member of the mesonychids, a family occasionally nicknamed "wolves with hooves." It had a massive skull, a long neck, and a deep lower jaw with grinding molars and strongly curved canine fangs.

SIZE Up to 5 feet (1.5 meters) long, weighing 400 pounds (181 kg).

FOSSIL HISTORY Originally named for its hooked fangs by J. L. Wortman in 1901, the genus is known from remains in Canada, China, and the United States. Remains from Big Bend are not conclusive enough to assign to a species.

The large, hoofed *Harpagolestes*. The specialized teeth of this primitive predator allowed it to crunch bone for the nutritious marrow inside.

BIG BEND FOSSILS Fossil teeth and jaws found in the Devil's Graveyard Formation by Margaret Stevens, James Stevens, and Jack Wilson in 1984.

DIET Carnivore and scavenger. *Stylinodon* and other smaller herbivores and carrion.

NATURAL HISTORY With inflexible limbs and a bulky frame, it was not an effective pursuit predator. It may have struck from ambush and bullied other predators off of kills. Skulls often show wear on the molars, suggesting that it regularly cracked bones to feed on the nutritious marrow inside. *Harpagolestes* was extinct in North America by the end of the middle Eocene.

Hyrachyus
(hi-Rak-ee-us)
("hyrax pig")
Order Perissodactyla
Family Hyrachidae
A small, swift rhinoceros. Physically resembling an average-sized, trunkless tapir with long, slender legs. A member of the hyracodontids (nicknamed the "running rhinos"), this genus was named for its piglike body. Its teeth resembled those of the hyrax, a small elephant relative with strong molars.

SIZE Up to 5 feet (1.5 meters) long and about 80 pounds (36.4 kg).

FOSSIL HISTORY The genus was discovered by American paleontologist Joseph Leidy in 1871. The species *Hyrachyus modestus* ("modest") was a small rhinoceros that existed only in the Eocene. It is an index fossil of the early Bridgerian Land Mammal Age.

BIG BEND FOSSILS Teeth and jaws collected by Margaret Stevens, James Stevens, and Jack Wilson in 1984.

DIET Herbivore. Like the present-day black rhinoceros, it had browser teeth and ate soft leaves, seeds, and tender branches and shrubs.

NATURAL HISTORY This ancestor of ancient and living rhinos and tapirs originated in Asia. *Hyrachyus* lived under the forest canopy and was preyed on by mesonychids and other primitive carnivores. It was probably a relatively swift little animal and may have moved in small family groups or herds.

Amynodon
(ah-Mine-oh-Don)
("threatening tooth")
Order Perissodactyla
Family Amynodontidae
A medium-sized, hippolike rhino. It resembled a large tapir, with

a short trunk, bulky body, and short robust legs. Both sexes had a broad mouth with tusks that flared outward, although males had larger skulls.

SIZE Up to 8 feet (2.4 meters) long and weighing 500 pounds (227 kg).

FOSSIL HISTORY Named by Othniel Charles Marsh in 1877, the species *Amynodon advenus* ("migrant") was an ancestral rhinoceros and an index species for the Uintan Land Mammal Age. It is the most common rhino found from this time period in Big Bend.

BIG BEND FOSSILS Skulls, bones, jaws, and teeth of at least eleven *A. advenus*, found at one Devil's Graveyard fossil locality. Collected by Margaret Stevens, James Stevens, and Jack Wilson in 1984.

DIET Herbivore. Browsed on soft leaves, flowers, and buds.

NATURAL HISTORY These rhinos had bone densities resembling that of modern, semiaquatic hippos, suggesting that they spent most of their time in swampy, tree-lined lakes and rivers, safe from predators. They might have emerged from the water in the evenings to browse. *Amynodon* survived into the early Oligocene.

Metamynodon
(met-ah-My-no-Don)
("after Amynodon")
Order Perissodactyla
Family Amynodontidae

A large, hornless, and semiaquatic rhino. Like *Amynodon*, it resembled the modern hippopotamus, with a barrel-shaped body; a short broad-snouted head; massive jawbones with large, forward-slanting bottom tusks; and smaller canines in the top jaw. Unlike hippos, it also had a prehensile lip.

SIZE About 13 feet (4 meters) long, weighing 3,968 pounds (1,800 kg).

FOSSIL HISTORY The genus was jointly described by William Berryman Scott and Henry Fairfield Osborn in 1887. In 1981 the species *Metamynodon mckinneyi* was named after Billy P. McKinney, who discovered the fossils on the Agua Fria Ranch. This species is known only in the Big Bend area.

BIG BEND FOSSILS Jawbone, canines, and teeth.

DIET Herbivore. Grazer and browser of grasses, soft plants, leaves, and flowers.

NATURAL HISTORY Like modern hippos, *Metamynodon* must have been a tough customer, using its powerful jaws and tusks to do fierce battle with rival males and predators. It likely grazed tough grasses during the night and spent the day in the water browsing aquatic plants. Also like modern hippos, the species likely served as a vector for redistributing nutrients from land into freshwater environments, fertilizing ponds and streams with its dung. Males had larger tusks, used to fight predators and other males for mates.

Megacerops
(Meh-gah-Ser-rops)
("large horn face")
Order Perissodactyla
Family Brontotheriidae

A massive, superficially rhinolike brontothere. Notable for the slingshot-shaped, meter-long blunt horns on its nose, which were much larger on males than on females. The horns were part of the skull; they were not made of keratin as modern rhinoceros horns are. The vertebrae on its neck were large, like a bison's, to support massive neck and shoulder muscles.

SIZE Up to 8.2 feet (2.5 meters) long, weighing a whopping 7,200 pounds (3,300 kg).

FOSSIL HISTORY Named by Joseph Leidy in 1870 from fossils

The enormous *Megacerops* Herds of these brontotheres were killed by volcanic eruptions of the time. Fossil herds were found by the Sioux, who assumed the animals would sound like thunder when running.

found in the northern plains states. There is a *Megacerops* fossil with a rib that healed after being butted by a horn, evidence that the males wrestled for mates or fought predators with their horns.

BIG BEND FOSSILS Brontothere fossils are rare in the Big Bend area, and the species is largely known from molars found in the Devil's Graveyard Formation.

DIET Herbivore. Browsers of tender vegetation and low-growing fruit. Attachment points on the skull suggest that a large tongue was used for stripping branches of their leaves.

NATURAL HISTORY The largest herbivore in its environment, a fully grown brontothere likely had nothing to fear from predators, since the predators were not as large as *Megacerops*. Like modern large herbivores, it probably played an important role in shaping the forests and plains where it lived. It was also found to migrate back and forth between North America and Asia. The group dwindled as the lush forests of the Eocene gave way to more arid savannas full of tough grass; the last of them vanished about 34 mya.

Epihippus
(ep-Ee-Hip-us)
("near-horse")
Order Perissodactyla
Family Equidae

An extinct genus of modern horse—a slightly taller version of the previous ancestor *Orohippus*. The Eocene Big Bend contained four-toed horses during the middle of the evolutionary transition from early horse to modern horse species. Modern horses have one toe on each foot, an adaptation that allows them to cover more ground to forage. Their five cheek teeth also evolved into bigger molars for more efficient grinding of tough plant material.

SIZE Almost 2 feet (60 cm) tall at the shoulders.

FOSSIL HISTORY *Epihippus gracilis* ("slender near-horse") was named by "bone wars" paleontologist Othniel C. Marsh in 1871.

BIG BEND FOSSILS Teeth fossils found in the Chisos and Devil's Graveyard Formations.

DIET Herbivore. Browser and grazer of grasses and vegetation.

NATURAL HISTORY Until the late Eocene, when they became extinct, these small horses were especially susceptible to the carnivorous predators of the newly approaching cooler grassland ecosystem.

Epihippus, a primitive ancestor of the modern horse. Its teeth evolved to eat from grasslands as forests disappeared.

Archaeotherium
(ar-Kay-oh-Theer-ee-um)
("ancient beast")
Order Artiodactyla
Family Entelodontidae

A predatory, rather hoglike ungulate with a long face. The robust 2-foot (60-cm) skull had the long cheekbones of a warthog and bony knobs around the head and face. The teeth had unique, thickly layered enamel, and they came in a variety of shapes: interlocking front fangs for stripping leaves off branches, enormous blunt canines for gripping prey, and flat squared molars used for cracking nuts and bone. The taxonomy of *Archaeotherium* lies somewhere between peccaries and hippos as well as whales.

SIZE The size of a cow, up to 6.7 feet (2 meters) long, almost 4 feet (1.2 meters) high at its humped shoulders, weighing 330–520 pounds (150–250 kg).

FOSSIL HISTORY Named by paleontologist Joseph Leidy in 1850, *Archaeotherium mortoni* ("Morton's ancient beast") was the largest species in its genus.

BIG BEND FOSSILS Teeth collected by Jack Wilson in 1986 in the Chamber Tuff Formation west of the park, which was deposited at the same time as the Devil's Graveyard Formation.

DIET Omnivore. An aggressive scavenger, hunter, and browser

Archaeotherium, the "hell pig." It had a huge head with cheeks like a warthog's, a hump on its back to hold up its big head like a bison, a large mouth, and snapping teeth. It also had a taste for camel.

of tender vegetation. Could not slice meat with its teeth but used its strong neck muscles to rip and tear chunks of meat from the bone.

NATURAL HISTORY This ungulate was one of the largest and most formidable predatory animals in its environment. The cheekbones and knobs on its head may have been used for display and in dominance battles. Given its huge jaw muscles and unusually wide gape, such battles could be lethal. One *Archaeotherium* skull shows healed puncture marks around the eye from another member of its species. It had an acute sense of smell, and it likely bullied smaller predators off their kills, as well as hunting opportunistically. Bite marks on contemporary camel skeletons suggest that it ran beside its prey, snapping at the prey animal's neck. One cache of fossilized small camels has been found with *Archaeotherium* bite marks in the bones, suggesting that the species was in the habit of storing food.

Specimens of young *Archaeotherium*, however, do not show the extreme jaw strength of sexually mature adults, suggesting that the powerful bite may have been as important in social behavior as it was in hunting—or that the animal's diet changed as it grew.

Texodon
(Tex-oh-Don)
("Texas tooth")
Order Artiodactyla
Family Homacodontidae

A small relative of the camel. It had a sleek body, long gracile legs, a long tail, and four hoofed toes on each foot. The teeth had crowns that were small, rounded projections instead of sharp-peaked cusps.

SIZE About 6 pounds (2.7 kg).

FOSSIL HISTORY The species *Texodon meridianus* ("southern Texas tooth") was named by Robert M. West in 1982, from type specimens discovered in the Devil's Graveyard Formation.

BIG BEND FOSSILS Additional teeth were collected by Anthony Runkel in 1988.

DIET Omnivore. Mostly herbivorous; may have also eaten carrion.

NATURAL HISTORY *Texodon* lived on the forest floor and was small enough to have many predators. Its speed and relatively small size may have allowed it to outrun or hide from threats, and specialized teeth could break up seeds and nuts. This small artiodactyl appeared in the early Eocene and went extinct with the cooler drier climate of the late Oligocene.

Leptoreodon
(lep-Tore-ee-Oh-don)
("slight mountain teeth")
Order Artiodactyla
Family Protoceratidae

A deerlike ungulate with short limbs. It had a mooselike snout, the low-crowned teeth of a browser, and the complex digestive system of a camel. It was an early member of the protoceratid ("first horn") family, a group of ungulates that eventually evolved slingshot horns on the nose.

SIZE Between 3 and 6 feet (1–2 meters) long, weighing 40–60 pounds (18–27 kg).

FOSSIL HISTORY Named by Jacob L. Wortman in 1898 from fossils uncovered in Canada and Texas. Three species were found in Big Bend: *Leptoreodon edwardsi* ("Edwards' slight mountain teeth"), *L. major* ("large slight mountain teeth"), and *L. pusillus* ("tiny slight mountain teeth").

BIG BEND FOSSILS Upper and lower jaw fragments with teeth found in the Canoe and Devil's Graveyard Formations. Collected by Margaret Stevens, James Stevens, and Jack Wilson in 1984 and Anthony Runkel in 1988.

Leptoreodon, a a tiny, hornless camel from a family that eventually grew slingshot horns on their snouts.

DIET Herbivore. Likely a browser of swampy vegetation around lakes.

NATURAL HISTORY Probably lived in herds in dense, brushy, and wet habitats. May have been quite comfortable in and around water as a browser, like the modern moose. This genus lived during the late Eocene, going extinct 37 mya.

Hyaenodon
(Hi-yee-Noh-don)
("hyena tooth")
Order Hyaenodonta
Family Hyaenodontidae

A predatory creodont mammal with teeth like a hyena's. It had a

Hyaenodon female with cubs. *Hyaenodon* had teeth like the feline hyena but was a canine ancestor.

large head with small, beady eyes and powerful, bone-crushing jaws. Its body was rather long, with slender, swift-running limbs.

SIZE Up to 5 feet (1.4 meters) long, weighing about 33 pounds (15 kg).

FOSSIL HISTORY The genus *Hyaenodon* was named in 1838 by paleontologists Laizer and Parieu and rapidly swelled to contain a vast number of species throughout North America, Europe, and Asia. Originally discovered in California, the Big Bend species *Hyaenodon vetus* ("old hyena tooth") was named by paleontologist Chester Stock in 1933. This species existed during the late Eocene (40–34 mya). Fossils of *Sinopa major*, another genus of this family, were also found in Big Bend.

BIG BEND FOSSILS Mandibles and teeth, collected in the Devil's Graveyard Formation by Jack Wilson and Margaret Stevens in 1986.

DIET Carnivore. Whatever it could grab and swallow whole or scavenge from other animals' kills.

NATURAL HISTORY A generalist predator, *Hyaenodon* was particularly adept at cracking bone. Fossilized droppings contain bits of skull from other animals. *Hyaenodon* and its relatives dominated terrestrial food chains in North America longer than just about any other carnivore, from the middle Eocene to the late Miocene, a total of 26 million years. Their persistence without specific predatory adaptations (their teeth were rather inefficient, and their paws were unable to rotate like those of modern cats) is a mark of their success. Ultimately, however, they lost out in part due to competition from more advanced carnivores.

·ᴄɢ 6 ᴐᴐ·

COOL FORESTS, DRYING PLAINS

The DELAHO, BANTA SHUT-IN, and
PLEISTOCENE FORMATIONS

DELAHO FORMATION
Latest Oligocene to Late Miocene
NALMA *from 24 Ma (Arikareean Age) to 16 Ma*
(Hemingfordian Age)
Time Traveler's Field Notes: *16 mya, April 9, 1:25 pm*
400 miles from the Gulf of Mexico

T HE SMELL IS OVERWHELMING. YOU ARE OUT ON THE LUSH
green plains of the Castolon, where a belt of spring storms
has raised a riot of fresh growth. All around you, as far as the eye
can see, the plains are packed with life. Herds of *Aguascalientia*
camels grunt and groan, grazing on fresh shoots, the season's new
calves, white-furred and woolly, prancing on wobbly legs. The
camels are the size of large llamas, and they mill with the easy,
casual lope of the very swift. As you walk through the cropped

grass, they keep an easy distance from you, watching with lazy, supercilious eyes. Their ears flick away clouds of biting midges.

These vast open plains are a new ecosystem in Big Bend, spreading out in a wide band across the slumbering, forested slopes of the Chisos and the flats on either side. Streams tumbling down from the caldera carry sediment to nourish the plains, and scrub brush and copses of spindly trees stand on the banks of the seasonal washes. Right now, some of those washes are flowing with muddy water, their banks whipped into a soup by a thousand narrow, sharp hooves. Some of the washes run in a network of cracks all the way up to the Chisos Mountains.

This sight resembles nothing so much as the modern Serengeti. The resemblance is only heightened by the presence of a pair of giraffe-sized camels, their velvety necks scarred and battered, lips curled back to reveal sharp canines. These *Delahomeryx* are the tallest herbivores on this landscape, and during the breeding season, males are viciously territorial with one another. These two circle each other, their necks arched to emphasize their height. Then they rush at one another, swinging their necks like battering rams, each trying to force the other down. Flesh and muscle slam together with meaty thumps, and breath whistles from their mouths, dust billowing from their pistoning hooves. Smaller camels scoot away, giving the battling giants room as they slobber and kick. Some of them wander closer to the wash, ears up, their calves wobbling along behind.

That is a mistake. A blur lunges up out of the bank, muscular flanks heaving. The camels react instantly, a few leaping into the air, others streaking away, grunting in panic. The calves streak away as well, nearly as fast as their mothers; but one, wrongfooted in the confusion, is not fast enough. A pair of heavy, tawny jaws close around its throat. The bone-crushing dog *Epicyon* shakes his head vigorously, then sits back for a moment, panting with exertion.

A hundred yards away, the smaller camels regroup, ears up.

But the *Epicyon* has his kill. Dragging the calf's body behind him, he slips back down into the wash that he used to sneak up on the herd, and he's gone. The herds of *Aguascalientia* are frozen in shock or mourning, ears back, limbs twitching in rapid waves, ready to flee at a moment's notice.

A shrieking groan is followed by a heavy impact. One of the *Delahomeryx* lands a particularly nasty blow on its rival. They break apart for a moment, panting, tails swishing angrily. Blood and saliva drip in strings from their canines. Then they close again for another bout. Around them the herds close back in, nervous and twitchy, to graze.

GEOLOGY OF THE DELAHO FORMATION

The transition between the Oligocene and the Miocene coincided with the final phase of the long growth of the Rocky Mountains, which—along with the retreat of the inland sea—was the defining process shaping the modern Big Bend. By the early Miocene (20 mya), the range had completed its rise, standing in bold contrast to the western plains below. For millennia, continental crusts had crushed against one another, forcing the mountains up. Now, with the compression tensions released, the crust of the North American Plate was left stretched and thinned across the width of the continent.

Seventeen million years ago, that crust began to crack and crumble in great blocks, creating broad basins and steep, high-cliffed ranges. This geographic region, which extends through most of the western United States, came to be known as the Basin and Range Province, a portion of which extends into modern Big Bend. (The Chisos Mountains now sit within the Tornillo basin, with the mountain ranges of the Sierra del Carmen to the east and the Mesa de Anguila to the west.) The resulting broken hillsides, basins, and slopes have defined the Big Bend landscape ever since.

In addition, a fundamental ecological shift took place, as the well-watered and dense forests that had long dominated the landscape gave way to open plains. During the early through middle Miocene (21–15 mya), the climate was warmer and drier than in the present. Ice caps began to form in Antarctica, dropping sea levels, while the rising mountains of the Cascades and Sierra Nevada in the west cast a rain shadow on the middle of the North American continent. All those events led to a much drier North American climate. As woodlands and their browsers shrank back, grasslands spread rapidly across the continent, including Big Bend. Carnivores and herbivores alike became larger and faster, and familiar mammal assemblages—grazing herbivores, pursuit predators—began to take shape.

The eroding Chisos Mountains—the remnants of an old supervolcano—had open depressions on either side, allowing water and soil to drain from the mountains and travel into the basin in a mixture of gravels, sand, silt, and clay, building up new fossil-filled formations. The erosion on the west side of the Chisos Mountains created the Delaho Formation, named after the Rancho Roman De La Ho.

The lower member of the Delaho Formation—pinkish, sandy siltstone of volcanic origin—is the oldest, and it has no formal name. Its fossils are known as the Castolon Local Fauna, which currently comprises around 22 species. The younger Smoky Creek member is named after a minor tributary of the Rio Grande, and it as yet preserves no fossils.

WHERE TO SEE THE DELAHO FORMATION

The Delaho Formation can be seen southwest of the Chisos Mountains starting at the Burro Mesa Pour-Off to the Rio Grande.

FOSSIL REMAINS OF THE DELAHO FORMATION
Reptiles

Among the multiple species of lizards and snakes that lived in the Delaho is one particularly notable reptile. *Geochelone* ("rock turtle") was a small land tortoise that somewhat resembled a modern Texas tortoise. The genus is known from shell remains throughout the formation, but it has not been assigned a formal species.

Small Mammals

By now large mammals had taken over the role of megafauna, but plenty of smaller animals made a living on the grasslands. They included two species of *Archaeolagus* ("ancient hare"), identified from a partial left jaw and molars by Mary R. Dawson, an expert in ancient rabbit fossils, in 1968.

The plains also hosted a specialized squirrel, *Similiscurus maxwelli* ("Maxwell's squirrel-like"), a ground-dwelling, seed-cracking, and grazing squirrel found only in the Castolon area of Big Bend National Park. It was named by Margaret Stevens in 1977 after Ross Maxwell, the park superintendent. Also present from the Castolon was *Gregorymys riograndensis* ("Gregory's mouse

The *Archaeolagus* genus of fossil rabbit. It came in a variety of sizes, as rabbits do today.

from the Rio Grande"), a pocket gopher that collected nest-building material (grasses and other vegetation) in its fur-lined cheek pockets, or pouches.

North America no longer has wild hedgehogs, but one was present in the Miocene Big Bend. *Brachyerix hibbardi* ("Hibbard's short cranium") was named by Margaret Stevens in 1977. Its body length ranged between 4 and 6 inches (10–15 cm), weighing 2 ounces (57 g).

Camels

Family Camelidae originated in North America about 40 mya, during the late Eocene. For much of that time, the family members were confined to the continent. They first appear in the Big Bend area during the time of the Delaho Formation.

The earliest camel ancestors were rabbit-sized herbivores. They had already evolved the high-crowned teeth and strong jaw muscles needed for chewing and grinding tough grass with abrasive sand grit. During the Miocene Epoch, camels diversified rapidly; they have been grouped into subfamilies by size and length of extremities. Species from several subfamilies are known from Big Bend. Among them were the early Miocene *Stenomylus crassipes* ("thick-footed narrow molar"), a small herding camel similar to a gazelle, about 2 feet (61 cm) high, with a small rounded head, a short muzzle, and a very elongated neck. There was also *Aguascalientia wilsoni* ("Wilson's of the hot waters"), a small camel with a long, narrow snout, along with *Priscocamelus wilsoni* and the tall, giraffelike *Delahomeryx browni*.

Oreodonts

A group of mammals unique to North America belonged to the Family Merycoidodontidae ("ruminating teeth") but were commonly known as oreodonts ("mountain teeth"). Resembling pigs, they were related to camels, with long heavy bodies and stocky legs. Each leg had four hoofed toes. They had tall, deerlike molars and short canine fangs. Very diverse in size and shape, the family included everything from semiaquatic browsers to cattle-sized grazers to clawed tree-climbers.

Miocene oreodonts in Big Bend include *Merychyus calaminthus*, a medium-sized ruminant with a hippo-shaped body found in Mint Canyon, California, and *Hypsiops leptoscelos* ("thin legs"), a grazer with high-crowned teeth for grinding tough grasses (it had thinner, shorter legs than any previously known species).

Originating in the late Eocene, oreodonts declined rapidly in the mid-Miocene, perhaps in response to the disappearance of swampy habitats in a colder, drier climate. An Asian migration of advanced predators into North America may also have played a part. They existed in North America for about 33 million years.

Mouse Deer

Nanotragulus ordinatus ("directed dwarf male goat") and *N. matthewi* ("Matthew's dwarf male goat") were relatives of modern mouse deer. They weighed between 15 and 38 pounds (7-17 kg), and they lacked antlers or horns. Their hind legs were longer than their front legs. There were four toes on each front foot and two toes on the back feet. Females were large; males had fangs that grew longer during the mating season. *Nanotragulus* species were frugivores first but ate seeds, flowers, leaves, roots, and insects for occasional protein.

Pronghorns

Members of the Family Antilocapridae, pronghorns are found only in North America. Their closest living relatives are giraffids, such as the okapi and giraffes. They have long legs, a long snout, and a short tail. The pronghorn has had many horn shapes in its history. As a grazer-browser, it would consume grasses primarily but enjoyed cacti, flowers, fruit, and berries when possible. Pronghorn jaw fragments with teeth are known from Big Bend, but not enough fossil evidence currently exists to identify particular species.

Only one modern species of pronghorn remains, *Antilocapra americana*, found in plains of the western United States, in the Rocky Mountains, and in West Texas near Big Bend National Park. Able to hit top speeds of 60 mph (97 km/h), pronghorns are easily the fastest living North American mammals.

Carnivorans

The Miocene marked the disappearance of many archaic mammalian carnivores and the emergence of early representatives of modern carnivore families, such as the Canidae, which gave rise to modern wolves and dogs. In the Delaho Formation, these were represented by the subfamily Borophaginae ("greedy eaters"), sometimes known as "bone-crushing dogs." Adept hunters and scavengers, their strong jaw muscles and huge bite force allowed them to crack bones to get at the marrow. The bear-sized *Epicyon haydeni* and the more primitive *Phlaocyon annectens* are the species of bone-crushing dogs found in Big Bend National Park so far.

Also present were the mustelids, the group that includes weasels and the largest family of carnivorous mammals. (Other mustelids are wolverines, badgers, otters, and ferrets.) In the Miocene, some mustelids, such as *Megalictis*, achieved sizes rivaling that of the bear-dogs.

Notable Species of the Delaho Formation

Heloderma
(Hel-oh-Der-ma)
("studded skin")
Order Squamata
Family Helodermatidae

A venomous lizard related to the modern Gila monster. Its stocky body was slow-moving. The tail made up 20 percent of the body length and was used for fat storage. Males had a larger triangular head with tiny eyes located in the broader region of the head. Its teeth were very small, widely spaced, and decreased in size toward the back of the mouth, with faint venom grooves on the lower teeth. The head, body, and tail had "beaded" skin, with large hexagonal osteoderm plates under each bead in the skin.

SIZE Up to 7 inches (25 cm) long, weighing 14 ounces (400 g).

FOSSIL HISTORY The genus *Heloderma* was described in 1829 by German zoologist Arend Friedrich August Wiegmann, who was the first to give the Gila monster a scientific name. Fossil remains of this family first appear in the Miocene. Fossils of *Heloderma texana* ("Texas studded skin") were collected and named by Margaret Stevens in 1977.

BIG BEND FOSSILS An almost complete skull with pearl-like osteoderms still fused to the cranium, along with teeth and vertebrae.

DIET Carnivore. Fond of reptile and bird eggs, frogs, lizards, insects, rodents, and carrion.

NATURAL HISTORY *Heloderma texana* was semiarboreal and terrestrial in the disappearing forests. The animals lived most of their lives in burrows, under rocks, or in thickets. Like its modern relatives, *H. texana* had modified salivary glands in the lower jaw that produced venom. Unlike snakes, it lacked the strong muscle attachments required to inject venom; instead, the lizard had to bite and chew to deliver the toxin. (Although modern Gila monster venom is toxic to the blood, people rarely die if treated quickly.)

Menoceras
(men-Nos-ser-rus)
("crescent horns")
Order Perissodactyla
Family Rhinocerotidae

Menoceras, a rhinoceros with crescent horns. Endemic to North America, it has been found as far south as Panama.

A pig-sized rhinoceros. Males had a pair of horns mounted on knobs on either side of the nose above the nostrils. These horns were made not of bone but of keratin—the substance that makes up hair and fingernails. Females were hornless.

SIZE Up to 5 feet (1.5 meters) long, weighing 515 pounds (234 kg).

FOSSIL HISTORY *Menoceras* has a complicated fossil history. Originally named in 1921, it has increasingly been synonymized with other similar rhinos, including "*Moschodestes delahoensis*," a new species discovered by Margaret Stevens in 1969 and found only in the Big Bend area. There is some question as to whether "delahoensis" represents its own species distinct from *Menoceras barbouri*, named after fossil rhino expert Erwin Barbour.

BIG BEND FOSSILS Upper and lower jaws; cheek teeth are

higher crowned than previously discovered in other rhinoceros fossils. The teeth were worn, fractured, or crushed.

DIET Herbivore. A browser of tender land vegetation and grazer of tough grasses.

NATURAL HISTORY *Menoceras* emerged from Europe in 23 Ma, during the last of the 14 million years of "rhinoceros rule," a period when rhinos were the heaviest North American mammals, before the later arrival of elephants. Occasionally occurring in mass graves, *Menoceras* roamed the American interior in large herds from New Jersey to Texas. The presence of horns on males suggests that they competed for female attention. Younger animals were likely picked off by bone-crushing dogs.

Ustatochoerus
(oo-Stat-oh-Keer-us)
("last hog")
Order Artiodactyla
Family Merycoidodontidae

Endemic to North America, the last oreodont before they went extinct in the late Miocene. With a large heavy body, long tail, short legs, and a long skull with canine tusks, it looked more like a rhino or hippo but was related to camels.

SIZE Pig-sized, about 220 pounds (100 kg).

FOSSIL HISTORY The species *Ustatochoerus leptoscelos* ("last hog thin legs") was named by Margaret Stevens in 1969. The fossils were widespread throughout the central and western United States.

BIG BEND FOSSILS Known from skulls, mature and subadult mandibles with teeth, and four-toed hooves.

DIET Herbivore. With crescent-shaped low grinding teeth, the same teeth seen on ruminants, especially camels. A generalized feeder eating any vegetation that was abundant at the time.

NATURAL HISTORY *Ustatochoerus* wallowed in swampy habi-

The oreodont *Ustatochoerus*. It has been called "ruminating pig," but it is more closely related to camels.

tats. Its species never specialized in grazing the new grasses of the changing ecosystem, and they never learned to run faster. They were outcompeted or were wiped out by the invading predators from Asia in the mid-Miocene; they existed for about 10 million years.

Priscocamelus
(Pre-sko-Cam-eh-lus)
("ancient camel")
Order Artiodactyla
Family Camelidae

An early species of camel rather like a gazelle, with long limbs and a shorter snout than its predecessors had. Its canine teeth were

Priscocamelus, a camel the size of a gazelle. It was endemic to North America before camels increased in size and migrated to the Middle East.

very large, sharp, and recurved toward the back of the mouth. It had high-crowned molars for grinding grasses.

SIZE Likely up to 3.2 feet (0.97 meters) at the shoulder, weighing 190 pounds (86 kg).

FOSSIL HISTORY *Priscocamelus wilsoni* ("Wilson's ancient camel") was named by Margaret Stevens in 1969 to honor Jack Wilson, the park's beloved paleontological fixture.

BIG BEND FOSSILS The species is known from a partial juvenile skeleton, front and hind limbs, metatarsals (bones connected to toes), maxilla and mandibles with teeth, and milk teeth.

DIET Herbivore. Grazed grasses and browsed high vegetation, such as leaves, tender branches, and fruit.

NATURAL HISTORY The large canines of these swift, herding camels likely figured in tussles within the herd. The long limbs were probably useful for kicking out at predators. Members of the genus may also have spit a noxious blend of bile, similar to modern camels and llamas. After its extinction, *Priscocamelus* was succeeded by giraffe-camels like *Oxydactylus* ("sharp toes") and *Aepycamelus* ("tall camel"), which had long legs and necks, reaching 18 feet (5.5 meters) and 1,600 pounds (700 kg). None of those larger giraffe-camels, however, are yet known from Big Bend.

Delahomeryx browni
(Del-ah-Hoe-mer-ix)
("Brown's ruminator of the Delaho")
Order Artiodactyla
Family Camelidae

A large species of giraffelike camel found only in Big Bend National Park. With long legs, an S-shaped neck, and true padded camel feet, it was smaller than modern giraffes but still quite large.

SIZE Up to 17 feet (5 meters) tall.

FOSSIL HISTORY *Delahomeryx browni* was named in honor of Perry Brown, the Big Bend superintendent (1963–1969) during the Castolon Local Fauna fossil collection. Fossils were found and named by Margaret Stevens in 1969.

BIG BEND FOSSILS Mandibles with high-crowned molars.

DIET Herbivore. Grazed on mostly grasses.

NATURAL HISTORY *Delahomeryx browni* lived in herds on the grasslands that were becoming predominant at the time. Its long neck may have been useful to scope out trouble and to browse from any trees it encountered. The species were likely swift runners and powerful kickers, which would have helped them evade predators.

Phlaocyon
(Flay-oh-Sy-on)
("greedily eating dog")
Order Carnivora
Family Canidae

A generalist bone-crushing dog, somewhat resembling a raccoon. It had a short, wide head and forward-facing eyes.

SIZE Up to 31 inches (80 cm) long, 4 pounds (1.8 kg), comparable to the smallest living modern canid, the fennec fox of Sahara.

FOSSIL HISTORY Originally identified and described in 1899 in Nebraska by paleontologist William Diller Matthew. It was considered an ancestor of the raccoon before it was identified as a canid in the 1940s. The species present in Big Bend, *Phlaocyon annectens* ("connected or joined"), lived there for about 4 million years.

BIG BEND FOSSILS Fragments of the mandible with molars.

DIET Omnivore. Small mammals, lizards, birds, insects, fruit, and plants.

NATURAL HISTORY Native solely to central and western North America, *Phlaocyon* existed in the Big Bend area from the late Oligocene (25 mya) to the early Miocene (21 mya). Like a modern raccoon, *Phlaocyon* likely was equally comfortable in trees and foraging on the ground, where its shearing teeth helped it make short work of small prey. It was likely preyed on by larger borophagids and giant mustelids like *Megalictis*.

Epicyon
(ep-EE-Sy-on)
("more than a dog")
Order Carnivora
Family Canidae

A bear-sized, bone-crushing dog. It had a short snout on a massive skull, a dome-shaped forehead, and enormous, powerful jaws. Its

The bottom jaw of an ancient bone-crushing dog. The structure of the jaw allowed the dog to eat every part of its kill. Front canine teeth were for grabbing, ripping, then tearing the flesh. Big carnassial teeth were for slicing through the meat and crushing bones. *Collection of the Panhandle-Plains Historical Museum, West Texas A&M University.*

very wide palate gave it room to chew large chunks of meat or joints of bone.

SIZE Up to 5 feet (1.5 meters) long, weighing 370 pounds (170 kg), making it one of the largest dogs ever known.

FOSSIL HISTORY Originally named by paleontologist Joseph Leidy in 1858, *Epicyon haydeni* was named for Ferdinand Hayden, a geologist who surveyed the American West, including Yellowstone, and found the first specimen of this animal in Nebraska in 1856.

BIG BEND FOSSILS Left humerus and upper jaw with partial crushing teeth and their roots.

DIET Carnivore and scavenger. Able to catch prey, crack bones for the marrow, and steal kills from other carnivores.

Epicyon, a large bone-crusher. It ate horses, camels, and rhinos, and also scavenged other predators' kills.

NATURAL HISTORY *Epicyon* was the last and largest of the bone-crushing dogs, and the dominant predator in North America prior to the arrival of big cats. Like modern canids, it was a pursuit predator, running on the tips of its toes and lengthening the distance it traveled between each step; however, it likely was not as fast as the modern wolf. Its hyenalike ability to break bones allowed it to access nutrients unavailable to other carnivores. The species *E. haydeni* existed in North America from the middle Miocene (21 mya) to the late Miocene (5 mya) on an arid savanna. Its extinction was likely due to changing climate and competition with other predators.

Megalictis
(meh-Ga-Lick-tis)
("giant wolverine")
Order Carnivora
Family Mustelidae

A large, short-faced mammal resembling a wolverine. It had short legs with nonretractable claws on each foot, and a long tail.

SIZE Estimated maximum length of 5 feet (1.6 meters) and weight of 130 pounds (59 kg).

FOSSIL HISTORY Originally named by paleontologist William Diller Matthew in 1907, *Megalictis ferox* ("fierce giant wolverine") is primarily known from South Dakota and nearby states, and also from Big Bend.

BIG BEND FOSSILS An unerupted premolar in a mandible fragment.

DIET Carnivore. Birds, fish, other mustelids, primates, and rodents.

Megalictis, a large mustelid. It belongs to the largest carnivore family on Earth today.

NATURAL HISTORY The size of this animal remains an open question, with some paleontologists estimating that it may have grown only slightly larger than a modern wolverine; others suggest it may have reached the size of a modern black bear. Either way, *Megalictis* represents an example of the variety of predators known from the period before cats arrived in the Americas. Able to climb trees and burrow with its powerful forelimbs, it was a tough, belligerent, and adaptable predator, likely waiting in ambush and grappling prey down rather than pursuing it.

BANTA SHUT-IN FORMATION
Late Miocene to Early Pliocene
NALMA
10.3 Ma (Hemphillian Age) to 4.9 Ma (Blancan Age)
Time Traveler's Field Notes: *8 mya, June 1, 12:00 am*
400 miles from the Gulf of Mexico

MIDNIGHT. A HALF-MOON HANGS OVER THE CHISOS MOUNTAINS, its light shining dim and silver over the savannas of the basin. The night is cool; crickets are calling in discordant choruses from the tall grass, and somewhere beneath a nearby log, something small and furry scurries out on its nightly rounds.

Even in the dim moonlight, you can tell that the walls of the sunken basin are steeper than the last time you were here, and the trees are fewer and farther between. The landscape is a little harsher, a little drier. The Rocky Mountains to the west are altering the continent's weather patterns, and so the grasslands of Big Bend grow golden and brittle in spring and early summer, awaiting the monsoons. Tonight marks the second month without any serious rainfall, and many of the wandering herds of herbivores have moved out of the basin in search of fresh growth.

Not all, though. Out on the plain, you can just about pick out the faint shapes of animals snoozing on their feet. A cluster of camels curl up like a scatter of boulders, their feet tucked under their bodies, necks stretched out along the ground. A few horses—somewhat squat and multi-toed—are grazing out in the dark, taking advantage of the cooler temperatures.

They aren't the only ones awake. A coughing moan carries up the slope, making the hairs on the back of your neck prickle and your legs quake. The sound comes seemingly from everywhere and nowhere, and you look around, fumbling in your backpack for the night-vision binoculars. The world snaps into green-tinted focus as you lift them to your eyes, scanning the tall grass. The call comes again, louder, but still lacking a clear source. Again you sweep the landscape, searching for movement. It sounds like the sort of call made by a big cat.

All at once, you spot it, a silhouette several hundred feet away, perched atop a bluff. It's the size of a large tiger, long-bodied, with spots that help to fracture its outline in the grass. This is *Nimravides*, a true scimitar-toothed cat and the top predator in the ecosystem. This one might be a female, roaring to advertise to roaming males that she's available; it might be a male, announcing his territorial claim. You don't see any cubs with it, so it's hard to say for sure.

Its eyes flash green as it turns to lope past you, the reflective lenses as flat and eerie as paper cutouts. Then the eyes move on. The head swings back to check over its shoulder, then back around to stare out into the dark. From somewhere out in the gloom, another coughing roar echoes like a distant shout. The big cat stiffens, posture going taut. It yowls, bobs its head, yowls again. Then, short tail cocked, it pads down the slope into the basin. You follow it with your binoculars until its shape fractures and melts into the grass.

The crickets call. The roars of the big cats roll out, sounding as if they come from both very close and very far away. And the savannas of Big Bend slumber on, silver beneath a summer moon.

GEOLOGY OF THE BANTA SHUT-IN FORMATION

As the Miocene gave way to the Pliocene, the grasslands and forests of North America grew chillier and drier still. The remnants of this shift are preserved in the Banta Shut-In Formation. Named by geologist James Stevens and paleontologist Margaret Stevens in 1985, it is exposed in the eastern half of the park near the three-sided Banta Shut-In, a corral of rocks used by pre-park ranchers to contain their cattle.

The Banta Shut-In Formation is a deep narrow gorge that was

created by the Tornillo Creek as it cut its way through a large intrusive sill of lava. The formation is primarily pink in color, made up of fine-grained pink sandstone, siltstone with a smaller grit, and red mudstone or clay.

Jim Liles, the chief ranger of the park in 1980, was the first to discover fossils in this formation. He reported his findings to Wann Langston Jr., the director of the Vertebrate Paleontology Laboratory at the University of Texas at Austin. After collecting some fossils of his own, Langston referred Margaret and James Stevens to the formation, which they named and collected from in 1980 to 1997.

WHERE TO SEE THE BANTA SHUT-IN

Take the trail from Estufa Canyon to Banta Shut-In, a 14.7-mile hike out and back. But be careful—it's a difficult trail. Also visit Comanche Ridge on the lower Tornillo Flat.

FOSSIL REMAINS OF THE BANTA SHUT-IN FORMATION

Reptiles and Amphibians

By the late Miocene and early Pliocene, many familiar genera of reptiles and amphibians had appeared in Big Bend, including rattlesnakes, toads, and whip-tailed racer lizards.

Camels

Camels remained an important and diverse component of the herds that ran through the Miocene grasslands. Camels of all sizes roamed North America, but because the area was so dry at the time, few fossils have been found in Big Bend.

By 6.5 mya, camels had migrated to Eurasia over the Beringia land bridge, and then to the Middle East and Africa, where they are commonly found today. *Titanotylopus* ("titan padded foot") and *Megatylopus* ("giant padded foot") are known to have lived in North America and migrated to Eurasia and then to Africa.

A million years later, another branch of the family went south as North and South America were joined by the land bridge we now call the Isthmus of Panama. There, they thrive today as llamas, guanacos, vicuñas, and alpacas.

Carnivores

Epicyon haydeni, the colossal bone-crushing dog, still dominated the grasslands during the early portion of the Banta Shut-In, alongside smaller predators like *Vulpes vafer* ("cunning true fox"), a primitive fox the size of a modern kit fox, which went extinct in the late Miocene. But change was coming. The first true dogs (like *Eucyon*) and true cats (like *Pseudaelurus*) were giving rise to larger, more advanced predators like wolves and saber-toothed cats.

Notable Species of the Banta Shut-In Formation

Crotalus
(Crow-Tal-us)
("castanet")
Order Squamata
Family Viperidae

A genus of rattlesnake that persists today. Members of the genus have pit organs located on both sides of the head, between the eyes and nostrils, which detect the infrared heat of warm-blooded prey. The fangs are long and hollow for deep penetration and injection of venom. They are hinged so that when the snake's mouth is closed, the fangs are parallel to the top jaw. Rattle segments are added to the tail each time the snake molts, and older segments wear out and fall off.

SIZE Up to 59 inches (150 cm) long.

FOSSIL HISTORY Modern representatives of the genus were

originally named by Carl Linnaeus, the inventor of modern taxonomy, in 1758. *Crotalus* is descended from snakes that came to the Americas from Asia during the late Eocene (40 mya).

BIG BEND FOSSILS Skull fragments and teeth.

DIET Carnivore. Rabbits, squirrels, rats and mice, gophers, and other small mammals.

NATURAL HISTORY *Crotalus* rattlesnakes are found only in the Americas, from northern Canada to central Argentina. They were and are ovoviviparous—the eggs are formed inside the female's body, incubated, and hatched before they leave the body—giving birth to live young. They are born with working venomous fangs and replace the fangs every 6–10 weeks. Like sharks, they have at least three pairs of teeth waiting to replace them. Rattlesnakes are shy but rather social as snakes go, often denning together with the same animals every winter.

Hemiauchenia
(Hem ee-Ah-Chen-ya)
("half-necked")
Order Artiodactyla
Family Camelidae

A camel ancestor of modern llamas, vicuñas, guanacos, and alpacas.

SIZE Up to 7.9 feet (2.4 meters) long, height 5.6 feet (170 cm) at the shoulder, weighing 882 pounds (400 kg).

FOSSIL HISTORY Originally named by French paleontologist Paul Gervais and Argentine paleontologist Florentino Ameghino in 1880, *Hemiauchenia* is known from multiple species from various areas in North and South America. The species for the western United States and northern Mexico was *Hemiauchenia vera* ("true half-necked"), but not enough fossil evidence exists to identify the remains from Big Bend positively.

Hemiauchenia, a llama-shaped ancestor of the camel. It was endemic to North America before it ventured to South America.

BIG BEND FOSSILS Jawbones with teeth.

DIET Herbivore. Browser of soft leaves and branches with fruit and berries first, before settling for grazing grasses.

NATURAL HISTORY *Hemiauchenia* lived on the open grasslands, among herds of grazing deer, giraffe-camels, and rhinos. In the manner of modern llamas and vicuñas, this ancestor likely ran first and spat bile later at predators, such as *Nimravides* and *Eucyon*. In the late Pliocene (3.5 mya) some *Hemiauchenia* migrated to South America via the uplift of the Isthmus of Panama. They were just one of many animals that headed south during this period, which is known as the Great American Biotic Interchange.

Eucyon
(Yew-Sy-on)
("true dog")
Order Carnivora
Family Canidae

A medium-sized canid.

SIZE About 33 pounds (15 kg), with a 7.8-inch (20 cm) skull.

FOSSIL HISTORY As described by paleontologists Richard H. Tedford and Xiaoming Wang in 1996, at least two species are known. The fossil remains from Big Bend are too fragmentary to confidently assign to a species.

BIG BEND FOSSILS Left jaw and teeth fragments.

DIET Omnivore. Small animals, plants, insects, and carrion

NATURAL HISTORY Arriving in the western United States in the late Miocene (10 mya), *Eucyon* was one of the earliest genera of true dogs to enter the fossil record; it persisted until the early Pliocene (6 mya). It is likely an ancestor of many modern varieties of dogs, including the modern coyote, *Canis latrans*. Like modern coyotes, it was probably a sociable and adaptable predator, occasionally preyed on by larger canids and big cats.

Pseudaelurus
(Soo-day-Lur-rus)
("false waggy tail")
Order Carnivora
Family Felidae

An early big cat. The body was long and slender, with short, strong legs and a long tail used for warmth and balance. The claws on its feet could retract halfway, and the upper canines slightly enlarged as the genus evolved. Each jaw had six carnassial teeth for cutting. Even larger grinding molars in the back could break down cartilage and bones.

SIZE The largest species grew up to 7.5 feet (2.8 meters) long, tail included, and a height of 26 inches (65 cm) at the shoulder, weighing 66 pounds (30 kg).

FOSSIL HISTORY Named by French paleontologist Paul Gervais in 1850, *Pseudaelurus* is known from multiple species found

Pseudaelurus, the last common ancestor of all living cats on Earth, including the extinct saber-toothed cats.

across Europe and Asia, including five from America. When describing the fossils of this cat, Margaret Stevens found them to be similar in size and shape to the mountain lion, *Puma concolor*. Fossil remains from Big Bend are too fragmentary to confidently assign to a species.

BIG BEND FOSSILS A right and left humerus, partial forearm bones, and toe bones collected by Margaret Stevens and her husband, geologist James Stevens, in 1989.

DIET Carnivore. An adaptable hunter and scavenger.

NATURAL HISTORY One of the first of the felids—true cats—to migrate to North America from Eurasia during the early Miocene (18.5 mya). Its arrival marked the end of the cat gap, a period of 7 million years in which no fossils of cats or catlike predators are found in the Americas. All modern cats and pantherines—as well as the extinct saber-toothed cats—are descended from *Pseudaelurus*. Its slender body and short limbs suggest that it was an agile climber of trees, which likely kept it from direct competition with and predation by other carnivores.

Nimravides
(nim-Rave-id-eez)
("nimravid-like")
Order Carnivora
Family Felidae

A large scimitar-toothed cat. Its canines were not as long or curved as those of *Smilodon*, so they fit more comfortably in its mouth, with some outside visibility when the mouth was closed. With a long powerful back and legs, this cat would chase down prey and execute a well-placed bite to the neck. The massive blood loss caused the animal to die quickly and saved the predator from injury.

SIZE Up to 6.6 feet (2 meters) long, height 3.3 feet (1 meter) at the shoulder, weighing 660 pounds (299 kg).

The feline *Nimravides* (also called *Machairodus*). Not to be confused with the Nimravidae, which were mammals that resembled cats.

FOSSIL HISTORY Described in 1958 by D. B Kitts, this genus is named after the unrelated nimravid family of carnivores, which resembled saber-toothed cats but were, in fact, more closely related to dogs. (The etymology of the name *Nimravus* remains unclear since Edward Drinker Cope never specified it, but it may refer to the biblical hunter Nimrod.) The species known from Big Bend is *Nimravides catocopis*.

BIG BEND FOSSILS An upper jaw with a partial canine, a molar the size of an African lion's tooth, a partial humerus, a big toe, and toe bones. The big toe fossil was longer and forked farther away from the foot than in modern cats.

DIET Carnivore. Young and ailing rhinos, camels, and deerlike mammals.

NATURAL HISTORY In the Americas, this saber-toothed cat coexisted with cougars, the American cheetah, the American lion, and jaguars, all of which have cone-shaped canines, the same as all modern cats. The scimitar canines were a powerful weapon for killing prey but were fragile; animals that broke them on bone would have faced a lingering death from starvation. They lived in North America from the middle to the end of the Miocene (10–5 mya), prior to the invasion of more specialized sabertooths from Asia.

Martinogale
(Mar-teen-Oh-gale)
("marten weasel")
Order Carnivora
Family Mephitidae

An extinct spotted skunk. It had a short broad face and a snout tip even with its large canine teeth. The long carnassial slicing cheek teeth and the low grinding molars enabled this skunk to eat a variety of foods. It had acute hearing and smell, but poor vision.

SIZE Up to 18 inches (45 cm) long, weighing 30 ounces (747 g).

FOSSIL HISTORY Originally named *Buisnictis* by its discoverer, Margaret Stevens. Renamed by Xiaoming Wang and colleagues to the present genus in 2005, it is now known as *Martinogale chisoensis* ("marten weasel from the Chisos Mountains").

BIG BEND FOSSILS A complete skull with lower jaw and teeth.

DIET Omnivore. Rodents, birds, lizards, snakes, insects, grubs, fruit, and carrion.

NATURAL HISTORY *Martinogale chisoensis* was very small and was similar in many ways to the modern spotted skunk genus, *Spilogale* ("spotted weasel"). It lived and nested in dark dens or cavities in rocks. It is not clear whether it had the scent glands that give skunks their distinctive odor, but it belongs to the family of skunks and stink badgers, as mustelids tend to be rather strong-smelling anyway. (It's what the name means, in fact.) This skunk lived through the Miocene, the Pliocene, and the beginning of the Pleistocene epochs.

PLEISTOCENE FORMATION
Pleistocene Epoch
NALMA
   from 2.58 Ma (Blancan Age) to 11,700 years ago
   (Rancholabrean Age)
Time Traveler's Field Notes: 100,000 years ago, November
   12, 4:25 pm
500 miles inland from the Gulf of Mexico

A SHARP WIND HOWLS DOWN THE GREAT WALLS OF SANTA ELENA
Canyon, whipping the muddy waters of the Rio Grande, whirling
white-capped waves against the slick limestone. Stands of conifer and hardwood trees rustle and clack in the breeze. Oaks and
cottonwood branches—stripped of their leaves by weather and
the turning seasons—toss against the sky. The forest is thick here
down by the river, fed by rich mud and alluvial soil carried by
the waters. The underbrush is covered in a thick, moist carpet of
decaying leaves. Shafts of golden light drop between the branches.

You hug your jacket closer around you, shivering. There is an
iron tang in the air, and your breath plumes in the afternoon sunlight. The air is full of the rush of water from the river. It is not
below freezing here, but the fall is slipping rapidly into winter.
This is the coldest temperature you have ever experienced during
your trips to Prehistoric Big Bend, and later this year it will likely
get much, much colder. On the slopes of the Chisos and the
higher plains, the wind is a cutting thing, racing across the plains
and marshes, carrying the bite of distant glaciers. Animals have
come down into the river bottom, crowding together to escape
the wind.

As always, posting up by the water is a good way to see them.
In the welter of tracks by the water's edge, you note raccoon, coyote, mountain lion, and even a great faded paw print of the saber-
toothed cat *Smilodon*. There have been multiple bands of horses

with striped legs, tossing their tails and nickering to one another as their hooves sink into the wet leaves. And you glimpsed a shambling, knuckle-walking ground sloth, all short shaggy fur and mud-encrusted claws.

The mammoths were the most impressive. They slipped out of the forest in surprising silence, immense elephants with long, curving tusks, standing thirteen feet high at the shoulder, sparsely furred and tan-skinned. Their trunks waved in step with their broad feet, and their small ears were held back against their sides. They clustered at the bank, steam billowing from their open mouths, curling their trunks up in quick gulps. Then, with a toss of the matriarch's head, they faded back into the forest. The scent they left—heavy, musty, not unpleasant—hung in the air after them, carried on the wind. Then that, too, was gone.

As the largest have disappeared, the smallest have come calling. Something moves in the leaf litter, quick and furtive—a tiny flash of gray in the shadows. For just a moment it pauses at the edge of a shaft of sunlight, bushy tail flicking, and you recognize it—a Mexican packrat. Its cheeks are stuffed full of seeds; it's not quite cold enough for it to cease foraging. Now it is headed back to a hole somewhere in the forest, beneath a boulder or a tree, where its midden is stuffed with twigs, bark shavings, and droppings, a warm and safe place to spend the winter.

It is so familiar, this view down the great canyon, and yet strange. Even with the bare branches, the forest around you is taller and thicker than anything on the river in the present day. One day the glaciers will retreat, and in the blink of a geological eye, the mammoth will be gone, and the horses, and the ground sloth. One day, the last traces of the forest will have shrunk back to the hidden valleys atop the Chisos and the preserved seeds of packrat middens. One day the sun will shine down on the rocks of Santa Elena Canyon as kayakers slip through turbid waters, into the shadows of limestone cliffs laid down by an ancient and vanished sea, and all the times you've visited will touch, just for a moment.

One day. But not today.

GEOLOGY OF THE PLEISTOCENE BIG BEND

Commonly known as the Ice Age, the Pleistocene Epoch stood at the end of a long trend of cooling that began in the Oligocene. During the preceding Pliocene Epoch, the world had changed markedly. Ice covered the poles in thick glaciers. Sea levels dropped due to the hardening of the ice. Major tectonic shifts resurfaced the Alaska-Siberia Beringia land bridge that connected Eurasia with North America, while North and South America were linked by a shift in the Caribbean Plate that raised the Isthmus of Panama, about 2.7 mya. Animals flowed across these land bridges, with mammoths, tapirs, and cats going south and armadillos, glyptodonts, and opossums coming north.

The Pleistocene saw further erosion of the landscapes of Big Bend, and the advance of vast glaciers down the American conti nent. Although Big Bend itself never froze over, cold winds blew down the continent from walls of ice. Sediments continued to erode on either side of the Chisos Mountains millions of years after the Delaho and Banta Shut-In Formations were deposited. These sediments were gravels that were not very fossiliferous, but elephant teeth were found east of the mountains.

Most notably, the Rio Grande (the bends of which give the park its name) was formed about 2 mya, as depressions in West Texas filled with sediment and eventually linked up to create a continuous flow to the Gulf of Mexico. The youngest river system in the United States, the Rio Grande makes up the border between Big Bend National Park, the United States of America, and Mexico. With its appearance, the familiar geological landscape of the modern park had finally taken shape.

WHERE TO SEE THE PLEISTOCENE FORMATION
Sediments from the Pleistocene can be seen at Estufa Canyon on the northeast flank of the Chisos Mountains. The area near Dugout Wells and its faultline has alluvium, a cover of loose sediment created by erosion during the last Ice Age.

FOSSIL REMAINS OF THE PLEISTOCENE FORMATION
Ichnofossils
Packrat middens are dunghills or garbage heaps of desiccated debris picked up by woodrats from their environment in the last Ice Age. The middens include plant material, vertebrate bones, and insect remains held together by sugars in the urine that dried and crystallized. This created an amberlike matrix that slowed the decay of the items collected by the hoarding rodents. The dry desert and frozen climate also slowed decay. Scientists have re-created ancient environments from the study of midden contents, which also included microfossils like pollen and spores. Big Bend National Park has one of the largest and most studied occurrences of packrat middens in America.

Notable Species of the Pleistocene Formation

Mammuthus
(Mam-ah-thus)
(Russian for "Earth horn")
Order Proboscidea
Family Elephantidae

A large North American mammoth. It had a single-domed head, a sloping back with a high shoulder hump, corkscrew tusks, a medium-length tail, and no fur.

   SIZE Up to 20 feet (6 meters) long with spiral tusks, 13.1 feet (4 meters) tall at the shoulder, weighing 22,000 pounds (1,000 kg).

Mammuthus columbi, with ever-growing spiral tusks. These were among the largest mammoths ever to live.

FOSSIL HISTORY Mammoth fossils have long been known from both Eurasia and North America, but the genus was formally named by British paleontologist Joshua Brooks in 1828. The species present in Big Bend—*Mammuthus columbi*—was named in honor of Christopher Columbus in 1857. The species is one of the most famous extinct animals in the world.

BIG BEND FOSSILS Tusk, jaws, and teeth. One rancher in the Big Bend area used the fossil mammoth teeth as a boot scrape before he was alerted to its identity.

DIET Herbivore. Grazer of grasses.

NATURAL HISTORY The mammoths lived around cienegas

(desert marshes), caused by seeps and springs in the American Southwest. These marshes or bogs were permanently saturated mats of sod with heavy surface vegetation of grasses, sedges, rushes, and reeds. The mammoths loved to feed in this squishy bog, but there was one drawback. A cienega was a hard place for any animal, especially an enormous one, to get out of once it became stuck deep in the mud. At least one mammoth died in this desert marsh, for one set of mammoth teeth was found in the park along with a tusk.

The Columbian mammoths of North America coexisted with Paleoamericans, such as the Clovis people who used the mammoth tusks for tools. Mammoths disappeared at the end of the Pleistocene, likely due to some mixture of changing climates and overhunting by ancient humans. Most mammoth species became extinct between 15,000 and 12,000 years ago.

Smilodon
(Smile-oh-Don)
("scalpel teeth")
Order Carnivora
Family Felidae

A tiger-sized saber-toothed cat of the Pliocene and Pleistocene. *Smilodon* had a robust body, but the spine and tail were shorter than those of a modern lion or panther. Its legs were stocky with smaller feet. It had a high scapula at the shoulders that moved up and down as the cat prowled after a hapless victim. The upper canines extended 7 inches (18 cm) or more below the lower jaw, and it could open its mouth at an angle greater than 90 degrees.

SIZE *Smilodon gracilis*, the smallest species, weighed between 120 and 220 pounds (55 to 100 kg). The species *S. fatalis* was 69 inches (175 cm) long and 39 inches (100 cm) high, and weighed 350 to 620 pounds (160 to 280 kg).

FOSSIL HISTORY Named by Danish paleontologist Peter Lund from fossils collected in the caves of Brazil, *Smilodon* was formally described in 1842. Subsequent North American species— *S. gracilis* and *S. fatalis*—were named in 1869 and 1880, respectively. It rapidly became one of America's most famous extinct animals.

BIG BEND FOSSILS A skull was among the fossils destroyed in a fire at the CCC-built museum in Big Bend National Park on Christmas Eve in 1941. The species was not recorded prior to the fire and remains a mystery.

DIET Carnivore. Large herbivores like rhinoceros and camels.

NATURAL HISTORY The eyes of *Smilodon* were smaller and did not face fully forward, which meant its three-dimensional vision likely was not as good as that of a modern predatory cat. This famous cat was an ambush hunter that concealed itself in high grass or bushes. How it killed is still debated, but with its prominent double-sided serrated teeth and the wide gape of its mouth, *Smilodon* could likely bring down animals much larger than itself with a vigorous bite to the neck. *Smilodon* died out at the same time as the Ice Age megafauna, perhaps due to competition with humans for dwindling large prey.

Gymnogyps californianus
(Gym-noh-jips)
("bare vulture")
Order Cathartiformes
Family Cathartidae

The California condor, a species of vulture, the largest North American land bird. Condors are uniformly black with a large triangular patch of white on the underside of each wing. The head is mostly bald with few feathers. When young, the skin is gray; it becomes yellow to a bold reddish orange as the bird matures. With gray legs and feet, condors have straight, blunt talons meant for walking, not gripping. Condors can live up to 60 years.

SIZE Up to 55 inches (140 cm) long, weighing up to 20 pounds (9 kg). Wingspan averages 9.8 feet (3 meters).

FOSSIL HISTORY In 1932, Frank M. Setzler of the United States National Museum (now the Smithsonian Museum of Natural History) excavated a cave in the Chisos Mountains for traces of ancient humans. Instead, he found the carcasses of California condors. Radiocarbon dating found that they had lived around 12,580 years before the present. Currently, these soft fossils are in the vaults of the Smithsonian.

BIG BEND FOSSILS Soft fossils of 27 desiccated condors. Desiccation is the state of extreme dryness far surpassing dehydration.

DIET Scavenger. Will travel up to 160 miles (250 km) a day to find carrion.

NATURAL HISTORY Condors prefer scrublands and coniferous forests. They nest in tall trees, cliffs, and caves and soar on the air currents in search of carrion. During the Pleistocene, condors were widespread across the Americas, feasting on the bounties of large carcasses spread across the landscape. Their population and range dwindled during the megafauna extinction of the last Ice Age. The International Union for the Conservation of Nature lists the species as Critically Endangered, with a few more than 500 individuals in the total population of wild and captured birds.

ACKNOWLEDGMENTS

ILLUSTRATIONS

All drawings are by Julius Csotonyi.

Most of the fossils photographed for this book were found in Big Bend and are in collections of the Texas Memorial Museum and the Vertebrate Paleontology Laboratory of the University of Texas at Austin. Unless otherwise noted, they were photographed by Cindi Sirois Collins in 2020 and 2021, with the kind permission of Dr. Matthew A. Brown.

PROFESSIONAL

Casey Kittrell: Thank you for having faith in this project and your contributions that helped move it forward. You have been consistently thoughtful and kind, making this process a wonderful experience.

Asher Elbein: Thank you for making this first-time author feel more at home in this scary business. You are a gifted writer, and it has been a pleasure working with you.

Julius Csotonyi: Your art is incredible to behold! Thank you for giving this book your time and your special paleontological touch!

Drs. Rick Giardino and Carolyn Schroeder of Texas A&M University and the Geology Camp for Teachers: You and your program changed my life and gave me the understanding and love of geology that led to my passion for paleontology.

Dr. Julia T. Sankey: Thank you for access to your research and for answering my questions. My communication with you was my first with a paleontologist, and because you were so kind, I felt comfortable reaching out to others.

Dr. Thomas M. Lehman, who spent decades in Big Bend National Park and is a paleontological rock star: Thank you, sir, for every detailed email that cleared up my confusion and for sharing your research with me. Your help and professional wisdom will always be a major part of the good memories of creating this book.

Donald W. Corrick, Big Bend National Park's geologist, and Steven L. Wick, the park's paleontologist technician, who wrote an unpublished, in-house fossil inventory of the park that I used *every day*: Don, thank you for this gift. Steve, thank you for sharing your wisdom and your research. Your help has been extensive and so appreciated. (*Note:* Qualified researchers can access this report by contacting Big Bend National Park, Division of Science and Resource Management.)

Dr. Sean P. S. Gulick of the University of Texas at Austin, a co-chief researcher for the Chicxulub crater expedition that found proof that the asteroid impact really did kill the dinosaurs and cause the extinction of animals of 60 pounds or more: Thank you so much for sharing your research and answering my questions.

Dr. Matthew A. Brown of the University of Texas at Austin Vertebrate Lab: Thank you for showing us the actual fossils I have been writing about for three years—such a great experience! Thank you as well for the information on the new *Quetzalcoatlus lawsoni*.

Dr. Thomas A. Shiller II of Sul Ross University: Thank you for your suggestions as you reviewed our book, for making geology terms clearer, and for the book blurb.

Dr. Judith A. Schiebout and her dad, Joe, who were all over Big Bend finding and studying the fossilized mammals at the beginning of the Age of Mammals: Thank you for sharing your memories in the park and for answering my questions.

PERSONAL

Bob and Joan Parriott: Mom and Dad, your devotion and guidance gave me the courage to take this leap. Thanks for your unending love and support.

My three sons, Beau, Ryan, and Wyatt, along with Beau's Lacy, Tatum, and Ember and Wyatt's Angelica: Hope you know how much you are loved and treasured.

Kaitlyn Simons, my sweet niece, who loves dinosaurs: Thanks to you and your parents for your love and support.

The love and encouragement of Jack the Elder and Miss Julia Collins and their wonderful family has meant so much.

Dale and Dot Namminga: Thank you, neighbors, for your friendship, wisdom on *so many things,* and news on the latest dinosaur discoveries.

Stacey DuVall, my BFF: more hiking and road trips in the future.

—Cindi

No book gets written without help. I'd like to thank Saul Elbein and Kayla Bennett for their support and advice throughout the drafting of this, Dr. Matthew Brown for being kind enough to welcome us into the UT fossil collections, and Cindi Collins for bringing me onboard this project and being an excellent collaborator. Onward and upward.

—Asher

SUGGESTIONS
FOR FURTHER READING

Csotonyi, J., and Steve White. 2014. *The Paleoart of Julius Csotonyi: Dinosaurs, Saber-Tooths and Beyond*. London: Titan Books.

Everhart, Michael J. 2017. *Oceans of Kansas: A Natural History of the Western Interior Seaway*. Bloomington: Indiana University Press.

Jacobs, Louis. 1995. *Lone Star Dinosaurs*. College Station: Texas A&M University Press.

Matthews, William H. III. 1960. *Texas Fossils: An Amateur Collector's Handbook, Guidebook 2*. University of Texas at Austin Bureau of Economic Geology.

Maxwell, Ross A. 1968. *The Big Bend of the Rio Grande: A Guide to the Rocks, Landscape, Geological History, and Settlers of the Area of Big Bend National Park, Guidebook 7*. Tenth printing, 2012. University of Texas at Austin Bureau of Economic Geology.

Prothero, Donald R. 2017. *The Princeton Field Guide to Prehistoric Mammals*. Princeton, N.J.: Princeton University Press. (Author has many prehistory books.)

Witton, Mark P. 2013. *Pterosaurs: Natural History, Evolution, Anatomy*. Princeton, N.J.: Princeton University Press. (Author is also a paleoartist.)

BIBLIOGRAPHY

Andres, Brian, and Wann Langston Jr. 2021. "Morphology and taxonomy of *Quetzalcoatlus* Lawson 1975 (Pterodactyloidea: Azhdarchoidea)." *Journal of Vertebrate Paleontology* 41(sup1):46–202.

Atkinson, Gerald. 2016. Big Bend National Park Cave and Karst Resources Summary. Cave and Karst Program, Texas Speleological Survey Natural Resources Stewardship and Science Geologic Resources Division.

Bell, Gorden L. Jr., Kenneth R. Barnes, and Michael J. Polcyn. 2013. "Late Cretaceous Mosasauroids (Reptilia, Squamata) of the Big Bend Region in Texas, USA." *Earth and Environmental Science Transactions of the Royal Society of Edinburgh.*

Bird, Roland T. 1985. *Bones for Barnum Brown: Adventures of a Dinosaur Hunter.* Fort Worth: Texas Christian University.

Busbey, Arthur B. III, and Thomas M. Lehman, eds. 1989. Vertebrate Paleontology, Biostratigraphy and Depositional Environments, Latest Cretaceous and Tertiary, Big Bend Area, Texas. Guidebook Field Trip nos. 1a, b, c. Society of Vertebrate Paleontology, 49th annual meeting, Austin, Texas.

Campisano, C. J., E. C. Kirk, K. E. B Townsend, and A. L. Deino. 2014. "Geochronological and taxonomic revisions of the Middle Eocene Whistler Squat Quarry (Devil's Graveyard Formation, Texas) and implications for the Early Uintan in Trans-Pecos Texas." *PLoS ONE* 9(7):e101516.

Cossette, Adam P., and Christopher A. Brochu. 2020. "A systematic review of the giant alligatoroid *Deinosuchus* from the Campanian of North America and its implications for the relationships at the root of Crocodylia." *Journal of Vertebrate Paleontology* 40:1.

Geological, Geochemical, and Geophysical Studies by the U.S. Geological Survey in Big Bend National Park, Texas. 2008. U.S. Department of the Interior *U.S. Geological Survey.* https://pubs. usgs.gov/circ/1327/pdf/Circular 1327.

Gulick, Sean P. S., et al. 2019. "The first day of the Cenozoic." *Proceedings of the National Academy of Sciences USA (PNAS)* 116(39):19342–19351.

Gustafson, Eric P. 1986. *TMM Bulletin 33*, Carnivorous Mammals of the Late Eocene and Early Oligocene of Trans-Pecos, Texas.

Lawson, Douglas A. 1975. "Pterosaur from the latest Cretaceous of west Texas: Discovery of the largest flying creature." *Science* 187(4180):947–948.

Lehman, T. M., and A. B. Busbey. 2007. *Big Bend Field Trip Guidebook.* Society of Vertebrate Paleontology, 67th annual meeting.

Lehman, Thomas, and Susan Tomlinson. 2004. "*Terlinguachelys fischbecki,* a new genus and species of sea turtle (Chelonioidea: Protostegidae) from the Upper Cretaceous of Texas." *Journal of Paleontology* 78:1163–1178.

Lehman, T. M., and S. L. Wick. 2010. "*Chupacabrachelys complexus,* n. gen. n. sp. (Testudines: Bothremydidae) from the Aguja Formation (Campanian) of West Texas." *Journal of Vertebrate Paleontology* 30(6):1709–1725.

Lehman, Thomas M., Steven L. Wick, and Kenneth R. Barnes. 2017. "New specimens of horned dinosaurs from the Aguja Formation of West Texas, and a revision of *Agujaceratops.*" *Journal of Systematic Palaeontology* 15(8):641–674.

Lehman, T. M., S. L. Wick, H. L. Beatty, W. H. Straight, and J. R. Wagner. 2018. "Stratigraphy and depositional history of the Tornillo Group (Upper Cretaceous–Eocene) of West Texas." *Geosphere* 14(5):2206–2244.

Lehman, Thomas, Steven Wick, and Jonathan Wagner. 2016. "Hadrosaurian dinosaurs from the Maastrichtian Javelina Formation, Big Bend National Park, Texas." *Journal of Paleontology* 1:1-24.

Lehman, Thomas, Steven Wick, Alyson Brink, and Thomas Shiller. 2019. "Stratigraphy and vertebrate fauna of the Lower Shale Member of the Aguja Formation (Lower Campanian) in West Texas." *Cretaceous Research* 99.

Lucas, Spencer G. 1989. *Coryphodon* (Mammalia, Pantodonta) from the Hannold Hill Formation, Eocene of Trans-Pecos Texas. University of Texas at Austin, Texas Memorial Museum, Pearce-Sellards Series 46.

Manchester, S. R., T. M. Lehman, and E. A. Wheeler. 2010. "Fossil palms (Arecacea, Coryphoideae) associated with juvenile herbivorous dinosaurs in the Upper Cretaceous Aguja Formation, Big Bend National Park, Texas." *International Journal of Plant Sciences* 171(6):679–689.

Maxwell, Ross A. 1968. *The Big Bend of the Rio Grande: A Guide to the Rocks, Landscape, Geological History, and Settlers of the Area of Big Bend National Park, Guidebook 7.* Tenth printing, 2012. University of Texas at Austin Bureau of Economic Geology.

Maxwell, R. A., J. T. Lonsdale, R. T. Hazzard, and J. A. Wilson. 1967. Geology of Big Bend National Park, Brewster County, Texas. University of Texas Bureau of Economic Geology Publication 6711.

Nydam, Randall L., Jacques A. Gauthier, and John J. Chiment. 2000. "The mammal-like teeth of the Late Cretaceous lizard *Peneteius aquilonius* Estes 1969 (Squamata, Teiidae)." *Journal of Vertebrate Paleontology* 20(3):628–631.

Paleobiology Database. www.paleodb.org.

Prieto-Marquez, Albert, Jonathan Wagner, and Thomas Lehman. 2020. "An unusual 'shovel-billed' dinosaur with trophic specializations from the early Campanian of Trans-Pecos Texas, and the ancestral hadrosaurian crest." *Journal of Systematic Palaeontology* 18(6):461–498.

Rowe, T., R. L. Cifelli, T. M. Lehman, and A. Weil. 1992. "The

Campanian Terlingua Local Fauna, with a summary of other vertebrates from the Aguja Formation, Trans-Pecos Texas." *Journal of Vertebrate Paleontology* 12(4):472–493.

Sankey, Julia T. 2001. "Late Campanian southern dinosaurs, Aguja Formation, Big Bend, Texas." *Journal of Paleontology* 75(1):208–215.

Sankey, Julia T. 2006. "Turtles of the Upper Aguja Formation (Late Campanian), Big Bend National Park, Texas." In *Late Cretaceous Vertebrates from the Western Interior,* edited by S. T. Lucas and R. M. Sullivan, 235–243. New Mexico Museum of Natural History Bulletin 35.

Sankey, Julia T., Barbara R. Standhardt, and Judith A. Schiebout. 2005. "Theropod teeth from the Upper Cretaceous (Campanian-Maastrichtian), Big Bend National Park, Texas." In *The Carnivorous Dinosaurs,* edited by K. Carpenter, 127–152. Indiana University Press, Bloomington.

Schiebout, Judith A. 1974. "Vertebrate paleontology and paleoecology of Paleocene Black Peaks Formation, Big Bend National Park, Texas." *Texas Memorial Museum Bulletin* 24.

Schubert, Joseph, Steven Wick, and Thomas Lehman. 2016. "An Upper Cretaceous (Middle Campanian) marine chondrichthyan and osteichthyan fauna from the Rattlesnake Mountain Sandstone Member of the Aguja Formation in West Texas." *Cretaceous Research* 69.

Standhardt, Barbara R. 1986. "Vertebrate paleontology of the Cretaceous/Tertiary transition of Big Bend National Park, Texas." Ph.D. dissertation, Louisiana State University.

Stevens, Margaret S. 1977. "Further study of Castolon Local Fauna (early Miocene) Big Bend National Park, Texas." University of Texas at Austin, Texas Memorial Museum, Pearce-Sellards Series 28.

Stevens, Margaret S., and James B. Stevens. 2003. "Carnivora (Mammalia, Felidae, Canidae, and Mustelidae) from the earliest Hemphillian Screw Bean Local Fauna, Big Bend National Park,

Brewster County, Texas." In *Vertebrate Fossils and Their Context,* edited by L. J. Flynn, 177–211. American Museum of Natural History Bulletin 279.

Stevens, Margaret S., James B. Stevens, and Mary R. Dawson. 1969. "New early Miocene formation and vertebrate local fauna, Big Bend National Park, Brewster County, Texas." University of Texas at Austin, Texas Memorial Museum, Pearce-Sellards Series 15.

Wagner, Jonathan R., and Thomas M. Lehman. 2009. "An enigmatic new lambeosaurine hadrosaur (Reptilia: Dinosauria) from the Upper Shale Member of the Campanian Aguja Formation of Trans-Pecos Texas." *Journal of Vertebrate Paleontology* 29(2):605–611.

Wheeler, E. A., and T. M. Lehman. 2000. "Late Cretaceous woody dicots from the Aguja and Javelina formations, Big Bend National Park, Texas, USA." *International Association of Wood Anatomists Journal* 21(1):83–120.

Wheeler, E. A., and T. M. Lehman. 2005. "Upper Cretaceous-Paleocene conifer woods from Big Bend National Park, Texas." *Palaeogeography, Palaeoclimatology, Palaeoecology* 226:233–258.

Wick, Steven L., and Donald W. Corrick. 2015. *Paleontological Inventory of Big Bend National Park, Texas: The Place, the People, and the Fossils.* Big Bend National Park, Division of Science and Resource Management, National Park Service, unpublished.

Wick, Steven L., and Thomas M. Lehman. 2013. "A new ceratopsian dinosaur from the Javelina Formation (Maastrichtian) of West Texas, and implications for chasmosaurine phylogeny." *Naturwissenschaften* 100(7):667–682.

Wick, Steven, Thomas Lehman, and Alyson Brink. 2014. "A theropod tooth assemblage from the lower Aguja Formation (Early Campanian) of West Texas, and the roles of small theropod and varanoid lizard mesopredators in a tropical predator guild." *Palaeogeography, Palaeoclimatology, Palaeoecology* 418:229–244.

Wikipedia and the Wikimedia Foundation.

INDEX

Tylosaurus (mosasaur), 17, 33, 34, 39–40, 44
tyrannosauroids (therapod), 18, 19, 90–91, 94
Tyrannosaurus (theropod), 58, 98, 115, 117
Tyrannosaurus rex (therapod), 7, 83, 90, 115–117, *116*

Udden, Johan A., 7, 23, 71
ungulates (hoofed mammals): artiodactyls, 124, 139, 149, 163–164; perissodactyls, 124, 139, 147, 148; predatory, 149, 161–163; true, 139. *See also* archaic ungulates
University of Texas (UT): at Austin, 8, 9, 189; at Dallas, 114; at El Paso, 7
urchins, 17, 26, 29, 42–43
Ustatochoerus (oreodont), 178–179, *179*

Velociraptor (dromaeosaur), 88, 89
Vertebrate Paleontology Laboratory (VPL), 8, 9, 189
volcanoes, 21, 146. *See also* supervolcanoes
volcanic ash, 3, 22, 41, 42, 144, 146, 147
volcanism, 22, 23, 42, 138, 146
Vulpes (fox), 190

Wagner, Jonathan R., 74, 109
Wang, Xiaoming, 193, 197
Wiegmann, Arend Friedrich August, 176
Weil, Anne, 54
Wellnhofer, Peter, 104
Wellnhopterus (pterosaur), 104–106, *106*
West, Robert M., 163
Western Interior Seaway (WIS), 15–17, *16*, 18, 25, 27, 30, 35, 38, 41, 46, 47, 50, 51, 56, 65, 72, 82, 93, 120
Whitaker, George, 127, 128, 129, 140
Wick, Steven L., 10, 11, 66, 70, 79, 91, 96, 107, 109, 115, 116
Wilson, John A. "Jack," 8, 9, 11, 127, 128, 129, 140, 146, 151, 152, 154, 155, 156, 157, 162, 164, 166, 180
wilsoni, 173, 180; *jackwilsoni*, 129
wobbegongs, 48
Works Progress Administration (WPA), 7, 44, 60, 74, 76, 79, 80, 81, 82, 86, 88
Wortman, Jacob L., 154, 164

Xiphactinus (fish), 17, 44–45, *45*, 50

Yarmer, Earl, 61, 65
Yehuecauhceratops, 58